# I Choose Life

# I Choose Life

Two Linked Stories of Holocaust
Survival and Rebirth

JERRY L. JENNINGS
AND GOLDIE AND SOL FINKELSTEIN,
WITH JOSEPH S. FINKELSTEIN

Library of Congress Control Number:            2009900305
ISBN:            Hardcover            978-1-4415-0306-0
                 Softcover            978-1-4415-0305-3

**To order additional copies of this book, contact:**
Xlibris Corporation
1-888-795-4274
www.Xlibris.com
Orders@Xlibris.com
58233

# CONTENTS

Map of Significant Locations..........................................................8
Family Tree..............................................................................9

Part I—Sol's Story....................................................................15

    Chapter 1.   A Good Life ...........................................17
    Chapter 2.   The Blood Red Moon ..............................28
    Chapter 3.   Descending ...........................................37
    Chapter 4.   Dante's Inferno .....................................42
    Chapter 5.   Death March to Mauthausen ....................47
    Chapter 6.   Depths of the Earth................................52
    Chapter 7.   From the Valley of Bones.........................61

Part II—Goldie's Story .............................................................75

    Chapter 8.   High Ceilings and Light...........................77
    Chapter 9.   A Child Alone .......................................85
    Chapter 10. Babylon...............................................90
    Chapter 11. Displaced Person....................................94
    Chapter 12. "Pick Up" Girl.......................................100
    Chapter 13. America ...............................................106

Part III—Epilogue ..................................................................111

    Chapter 14. Chicken Farmers....................................113
    Chapter 15. An Extraordinary Deliverance .................118

Afterword.............................................................................123
A Note From the Writer ........................................................129
Timeline of Historical Events ................................................132
Acknowledgements ...............................................................141

Sol Finkelstein and Goldie Cukier Finkelstein dedicate this book
to the memory of our parents and siblings
Jacob, Golda, Abraham, Aaron, Ann and Joseph Finkelstein
and
Joseph, Miriam, Toby, Ateek and Gucia Cukier
and
in honor of our grandchildren
Adam, Julie, Seth, David and Ilana Finkelstein

Contact Information:

Joseph S. Finkelstein at: *jsfink@aol.com*

Jerry L. Jennings at: *jerryj100@comcast.net*

*www.ichooselifebook.com*

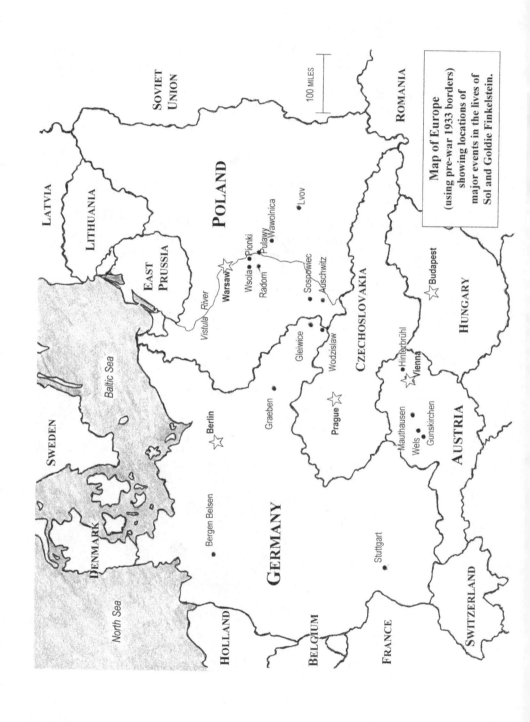

Map of Europe
(using pre-war 1933 borders)
showing locations of
major events in the lives of
Sol and Goldie Finkelstein.

100 MILES

SOVIET
UNION

LATVIA

LITHUANIA

EAST
PRUSSIA

POLAND

Vistula River

Warsaw

Wsola • Pionki
Radom • Pulawy
• Wawolnica

• Lvov

Sospowiec
Auschwitz

Gleiwice

Wodzislaw

CZECHOSLOVAKIA

Prague

Graeben

Berlin

Baltic Sea

SWEDEN

DENMARK

North Sea

Bergen Belsen

GERMANY

Stuttgart

HOLLAND

BELGIUM

FRANCE

SWITZERLAND

AUSTRIA

Mauthausen
Wels • Gunskirchen

Vienna
• Hinterbrühl

HUNGARY

Budapest

ROMANIA

# Finkelstein Family Tree

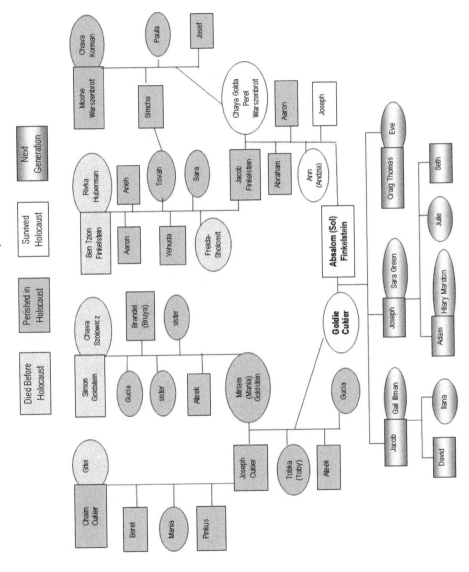

*I have put before you life and death, blessing and curse.*
*Choose Life—so that you and your descendants will live.*
*Deuteronomy 30:19*

*I have opened your graves, and lifted you out of your graves.*
*I will put breath into you and you shall live again.*
*Ezekiel 37:13-14*

*"A sane person cannot imagine what it was like . . . ."*

—*Sol Finkelstein*

# Part I
## Sol's Story

# CHAPTER ONE

# A Good Life

I was born in Poland on September 16, 1925, on the first day of Rosh Hashanah, the Jewish New Year. For a religious family like mine, it was a blessing to be born on such a holy day. It is said that Abraham, Isaac and Jacob were all born on Rosh Hashanah. Not that I'm in their league, but maybe this was God's way of saying that He had something special planned for me. I believe so. If He had not saved me so many times, I would not be here to tell my story now.

My name is Sol Finkelstein. It is a tradition among Jews to name a child after a deceased loved one. My older brothers Abraham, Aaron and Joseph had already taken the names of our only dead relatives, so my parents picked a Biblical name for me, "Absalom." In Hebrew, it's Avshalom. He was the oldest son of King David, the one who betrayed his father and was defeated when his beautiful, long hair became entangled in a tree. "Sol" comes from Absalom. "Sol" is what everyone has always called me.

My first years were spent in Pulawy, a town on Poland's largest river, the Vistula, about 60 miles south of Warsaw. My mother, Chaya Golda Perel Warszenbrot, grew up in Pulawy, and my father, Jacob Noah Finkelstein, was born in a neighboring town called Konskowola and grew up in nearby town known as Wawolnica.

My parents had an arranged marriage as was common practice for Jewish families in those days. They first met at a family wedding when they were young children, just seven or eight years old. My mother was the kid sister of the groom, Simcha Warszenbrot, and my father was the kid brother of the bride, Tovah Finkelstein. And when the *machatunim* saw this, they decided right then and there, "These two will be a couple." It was fated. I don't know if my parents ever saw each other again before they married, but the *shidekh*, the match, was made at the wedding that very day. Of course, when one brother and sister marry each others' brother and sister, it leads to confusion, so there were many family jokes about our double relations. For instance, it meant that my Uncle Simcha was my mother's brother and my aunt's husband. And my aunt Tovah was my father's sister and my uncle's wife. You get the picture.

When my parents married, my mother was already a successful young businesswoman. Smart and capable, she owned and operated her own grocery store in Pulawy. My father, on the other hand, had been a poor *yeshive bucher*, a student in the famous Jewish religious academy in Lublin. He wanted to be a Talmudic scholar, but my mother insisted that this was no way to support a family. "You have to make a living for me and the children." She knew it would hurt business with the Poles if Father looked too Orthodox so she cut off his long Jewish beard and ear-locks. Father went to work with Mother in her grocery business, but he remained very observant and continued to *daven*, pray, every day.

Years later, as I came along and the Finkelstein family grew to five children, my parents looked beyond Pulawy for better economic opportunities. When I was about three years old, they sold the little grocery and moved to Radom about 35 miles to the west. Compared to Pulawy, Radom was a large commercial city of 150,000 people with a thriving Jewish community of 35,000. There my father was a *voyageur*, a traveling salesman, selling goods as the exclusive agent in Poland for a chocolate manufacturer in Lvov.[1] My father traveled all over Poland by rail, which was the main method of transportation in those days, to sell chocolates to various wholesalers and stores. My mother's domain was the house and the children. It was a demanding job for her because Father was on the road every week. He gave my mother the money, and she took care of everything.

I don't recall a single argument between my mother and father. Everybody in our family got along, even the kids. In those days, if there was a problem that the family couldn't handle, you would go see the *Rebbe*, the Rabbi. For a religious Jewish family like ours, the Bible had an answer for every question and whatever the *Rebbe* advised, it was always the right advice.

My first memories begin in Radom where *Yiddishkeit*, Jewishness, touched every aspect of my life. My earliest recollections are of an affectionate Jewish home, full of joy and Hebrew songs, with pictures of Jewish leaders on the walls, and chatter about Zionism and Israel around the table. Both of my parents had very religious fathers, and though our home was not as observant as theirs, we

---

[1]     Lvov is also translated as Lviv and Lwow. It was then part of Poland, today it is located in the Ukraine.

were thoroughly Jewish. In those days in Poland, there was not much variation in Jewish observance like there is today. You ate kosher food, you got up in the morning and put on *tallis* and *tefillin* to pray, you went to synagogue faithfully. And the Sabbath was absolutely sacred—no driving, no working whatsoever. That was our life. There was no thought of why or what you did. Your father put on *tefillin*, your brothers put on *tefillin*, you put on *tefillin*. As a Jew, it was all you knew. There were very few Jews in Poland in those days that were not kosher and they were frowned upon for it.

Clothing was the most visible difference between regular observant Jews, like my family, and the extremely observant Orthodox Jews. An Orthodox Jew always wore a black *yarmulke* (skull cap), a long beard, *peyes* (earlocks), long black clothes, and a *tallis katan* with the *tzitzit* (fringes) dangling in sight. We never wore the Orthodox clothing—except when we visited my grandfather Moshe back in Pulawy.

Grandpa Warszenbrot was short and thin, maybe five feet tall and ninety pounds, but he was strong like an ox. I'll always remember his weak beard. When he was young, he was attacked by the Chmielnitskis. These were marauding bands of Ukrainian soldiers who invaded Poland at the end of World War I to spread Bolshevism. They took their name from General Chmielnitski, whose Cossacks fought against the Poles in 1648 and massacred tens of thousands of Jews. The Chmielnitskis hated Jews and they grabbed my poor grandfather. They set fire to his proud Jewish beard and laughed. Grandfather bore the burn scars on his face and could only grow a meager beard in its place. But this never bothered him. He said, "It could not have been any different. If God meant it any different, He would have never sent the Chmielnitskis to Pulawy." Grandfather had unquestioning faith in God. He believed that whatever happens, even a terrible event, happens because God wants it to happen. For Grandfather, great troubles were a test of your true belief—like God tested Job to see if he would stay faithful, or tested Daniel in the lion's den or Jonah in the belly of the whale.

Grandfather's unquestioning faith was not unique to him. It is a typically Orthodox Jewish perspective. It shows the intensity of his piety and why he was determined to correct our ways when we stayed with him in Pulawy in the summertime. Grandpa would quiz me about the Torah and scold me if I did not get up in the morning to *daven*. He insisted that I wear a *yarmulke* and *tallis katan* at all times. The *tallis katan* is basically a prayer shawl in the form of a sleeveless garment that goes over your head and is worn under your shirt. It displays the knotted tassels called *tzitzit* at your waist, which show your obedience to God's commandments.

At Grandfather's house, I had to *daven* every morning. I knew the prayers well, but it is not so easy to pray in the morning when you're young and your stomach is growling. You're not supposed to eat before you *daven* so Grandma

(Chava Korman Warszenbrot) would sneak me a little bit of breakfast before Grandpa saw me. That's a grandmother for you—a smile, a pinch on the cheek, a piece of candy. Grandma was round and chubby, always smiling, and she always wore a *sheitel*, a wig. I still remember her soft round face with cute cheeks and sparkling eyes. Her house and her heart were big enough for all of her many grandchildren.

My grandfather made his living as a *jobber*. That is Yiddish for a middle man who purchases goods from one vendor and then resells the goods to another vendor. Grandpa's business was buying produce from farmers. He would buy a crop of strawberries or apples or pears, then harvest them, package them, and send them to Warsaw for sale.

My family would also go to visit my mother's oldest brother, Uncle Simcha. He was a big man with a chest like a bear and a beard that reached his knees. He was so strong that I thought he would kill me when he hugged me, which was often. Uncle Simcha was so bright and learned in Torah that he was an advisor to Rabbis. He had many children and they all lived on a sort of farm in a tiny *shtetl* called Wawolnica. If you yawned, you missed it. We were related by blood to almost half of the town of Wawolnica.

For a city boy from Radom, the *shtetl* was an exciting place to visit. It was so primitive. There were no cars. The peasants rode horses bareback and drove horse-drawn wagons. There were cows and livestock making noises. The houses were small wooden buildings with thatched roofs. In the center of the *shtetl*, there was a tiny market square with maybe ten buildings and a Jewish store in each one. You pumped your water from a well and used an outhouse because there was no plumbing. There was no electricity in the *shtetl* either. I remember one of my cousins once came to visit us in the city. We had a radio playing and he ran from our apartment, screaming, "A *dybbuk*! A *dybbuk*!" He had never seen a radio before. He thought our home was possessed by evil spirits and that Satan was talking to him out of the box! That's how different our city life was from peasant life in the *shtetl*.

My mother had two brothers, Simcha and Josef, and one sister, Paula. My father was the youngest of seven children, four boys and three girls: Aaron, Arieh, Tovah, Yehuda, Sara, Frida-Shlomit and finally my father—Jacob. So I had aunts and uncles here and aunts and uncles there. And, of course, cousins and more cousins. The only relative who lived nearby was my mother's youngest brother, Josef Warszenbrot. Uncle Josef would come over on the Sabbath and play chess for hours. He especially liked to play with me because he had no sons of his own, just two daughters. The rest of our extended family was spread all over Poland with a few living in Israel. Like the diversity of Polish Jewry itself, we had relatives living in big cities like Warsaw, which had hundreds of thousands of Jews, to smaller cities like Radom where I grew up, to small towns and tiny *shtetls* like Wawolnica where Uncle Simcha lived. In the years before the war, there were thousands of Jewish communities in Poland, big, medium and small. Today, there's nothing.

My immediate family was four boys and a girl. I was the *mizinik*. That is Yiddish for the youngest child. My oldest brother Abraham was about 8 years older than me. Then there was my brother Aaron, my sister Ann (Chana), my brother Joseph, and me. When I was five, my father predicted careers for all of us. He said Abraham would be a doctor or a scientist because he was so brilliant. Aaron would be an accountant because he was a genius in mathematics. Ann would be a dancer because she was very good in ballet. And he told me that I was destined to be a lawyer. I forget what he predicted for Joseph. Unfortunately, the war destroyed all of his predictions, but maybe his wishes came true because my own son Jacob became a doctor, and my son Joseph became a lawyer.

In Radom, we lived in a spacious apartment on the third floor of a large apartment building with four stories. The address was 26 Pierackiego Street, which was named after a former Polish premier.[2] We had a small balcony that overlooked busy Pierackiego Street. Like many places in Poland, our apartment building was connected to other buildings in a continuous perimeter that formed a square and nearly covered a full city block. Inside the square was a nice courtyard where we could play. There were about a hundred tenants in our building, nearly all Jewish, because Jews tended to congregate with other Jews in Poland. We would enter from Pierackiego Street through a gateway into the courtyard. A public school named after a Polish Jewish hero, Joselowicz, was on the left side and our apartment was on the right.

My typical day would begin with a long walk to school, which was a little over a mile. There were no buses or trolleys, so we walked summer and winter. School started at 8 a.m. and finished at 2 p.m. The school usually provided lunch, but sometimes we brought food from home. When we returned home in the afternoon, our family would have its main meal for the day. In Poland, people would eat their supper during the day. Then it was time to do homework. In our home, homework was as important as religion. You never did anything until your homework was done.

I liked school. Like most Jewish boys, I started *Cheder* when I was five. The *Cheder* was a Jewish secular school, but the emphasis was on Jewish learning and Hebrew. Everybody but the janitor was Jewish. Boys and girls attended together and I had a lot of friends. A Jewish religious school teacher is called the *Melamed*. If you didn't pay attention, or you didn't know the answer quickly enough, the *Melamed* would smack you on the knuckles! That was how we

---

[2]  In modern day Poland, the street has been renamed Niedzialkowskiego Street.

learned. We were taught to read and speak Hebrew. We studied the traditional Jewish prayers, *Chumash, Rashi*, and a little bit of *Gemorah*. But we also studied secular subjects like science, Latin, German, mathematics, and history. As much as we wanted to learn all about the world, we could never forget that we were Jewish.

I think I was nine years old when I graduated from the *Cheder*. The secondary school had an odd name, "Friends of Knowledge" (*Przyjaciol Wiedzy*). It was also a Jewish secular school and parents had to pay tuition to send their children there. Our education mixed secular subjects with more advanced Hebrew, *Tanach, Mishneh*, and *Gemorah*. We had separate teachers for each Jewish subject and for each secular subject. Most of the teachers were old maids and they often had their favorites. I was the favorite of the German teacher. She was maybe four feet tall. I was a small boy but I was still taller than her.

My older brothers were such brilliant students that the teachers expected a lot from me. I always lived in the glory of how well Abraham and Aaron did. A teacher once said to me, "Sol, you have big shoes to fill, because Abraham was in my class, and Aaron was in my class." I was expecting her to make the usual comparison, but she surprised me. "Ah, but you're doing well, Sol, you're filling those shoes." So I guess I was pretty smart too. I read a lot. In fact, I was an assistant librarian in the school, which exposed me to every kind of book. I didn't understand many of the books I read, but I read them nonetheless, and reread them. Some of it stuck. Some of it didn't.

After homework was done, we were free to play. Sometimes I played outside with friends, but mostly I would follow my older brothers and sister to the Zionist youth clubs. There were several to choose from in Radom. *HaShomer Ha'tzair* was politically left, *Beitar* was right and there was *Mizrachi* for the very religious. The politics of each did not matter so much to me. Personally, I liked *HaShomer Ha'tzair* because the girls were prettier. They all offered the same kind of camaraderie and fun, and each one taught the same passionate love of Israel and Zionism. We would sing Hebrew songs and dance *horas* and march about. Then, at about 6:30, everyone would go home, eat a sandwich and go to sleep. Life was simple and sedate.

You see, for Jews in Poland, the dream of a Jewish homeland was supremely important. From the earliest I could remember, there was talk of Israel and the belief that Zionism would revitalize the Jewish people. We all dreamed that someday we would see a land of Israel. That was the thing we always talked about at our table. We sang Zionist songs and read Zionist literature. We all wanted to go to Jerusalem. *Yerushalayim shel zahav*. Jerusalem of gold. As we learned from Psalm 137, a Jew must never forget his connection to Jerusalem or he will be lost.

The love of Jerusalem and Israel permeated our traditional prayers. Even the daily morning prayer says, *"Tolichenu kommiyut l'artzenu."* It means we should return upright, in dignity, to our homeland. I felt Zionism strongly because it was all around me. My father was a passionate Zionist. So, too, were my older brothers and sister, and my mother. We all believed in Zionism. My grandfather's absolute greatest wish was to go to Israel and be buried in Jerusalem.

As Jews, I think we always dreamed about Israel because we never felt safe in Poland. There were millions of Jews living in Poland. Some were well off, but a great many more were very poor. And we were always hated by the Poles. Poland never felt like our home country. No matter how successful you were in Poland, no matter how many generations your family lived there, if you were a Jew, you were still an outsider. That's why we always talked about an independent land of Israel. The modern Zionist movement first started in the 1870s and grew popular because the Jews in Poland never felt that they belonged there—even after living there for 900 years.

In Poland, there was no hiding that you were a Jew, especially if you wore the clothes and beard of an Orthodox Jew. The Poles were blond and fair-skinned and we Jews were mostly dark. Anti-Semitism was an everyday occurrence. For children, it took the form of taunts and racist slurs. When we walked to and from school, the Polish boys would often yell, "dirty Jew" or "filthy Jew" or throw stones at us. Sometimes they would threaten to beat us up and chase us. But that is as far as it went. Later, as Hitler and the Nazis became more powerful in the late 1930's, the Polish anti-Semites also became louder and bolder. A few started to break windows in Jewish stores and bully Jews on the street. But, for the most part, anti-Semitism was an irritation that we were accustomed to, like a stone in your shoe.

Like most Jews, of course, our weekends were centered on *Shabbat*, the Sabbath, which started at sundown on Friday evening and ended at sundown on Saturday. Father would return home from his business trips each Thursday afternoon so that he would never have to travel on the Sabbath. He wanted to be ready for Friday night like everyone else. Thursday was also the day when the *schnorrers* would come to our house. They were Jewish beggars and it was traditional to treat them with charity and kindness. The *schnorrers* would make the rounds in the neighborhood, visiting certain houses at certain times. Our day was Thursdays. My mother would always give the *schnorrers* a prepared meal and a few coins of *tzedakah*, charity. The *schnorrers* knew who would give and who wouldn't. My mother always had an open door and always gave. She honestly believed that the more she gave, the more God gave to her. I think it's true, too.

Then it was Friday. Friday was very traditional. The women went to the *mikvah* on Friday morning to cleanse themselves, the men washed up in the late afternoon, and everybody dressed in fine clothes to walk together to synagogue in the evening. After services, we all walked home and the family would gather around the table to eat and sing *z'mirahs*, Hebrew songs. Then, after the meal, we all *bentsched* (recited prayer blessings) and talked about Israel and Zionism.

Saturdays were always the same. In the morning we all walked to synagogue to *daven* again. Then the afternoon would be lazy and relaxed, a true day of rest as God intended. The children went out to play and the adults went to visit friends and relatives who lived within walking distance.

Then Sunday would come and Father would pack his suitcase to start another week of traveling sales.

As the youngest in the family, I felt that we had the perfect life in Radom. I had a loving family with lots of hugging and kissing. We were well-educated and comfortably middle-class. I had many good friends. We lived in a Jewish neighborhood, spoke Jewish, went to Jewish school, *davened* every day, and dreamed of a Jewish homeland. We enjoyed a passionate and satisfying Jewish life. The Torah was the basis of our life as it had been for Jews for 3,000 years. Simple truths like, "Love thy neighbor as thyself." "Thou shall not kill; thou shall not steal; thou shall not covet." "Honor your parents." It is all in the Bible. To have a good life, all you have to do is be a good person and respect others.

I have only happy recollections from my young childhood—memories of how we marched and sang, how we played, how I went to school, how my oldest brother taught me to ride a bike during our summer family vacation. There was only one time that was upsetting. My oldest brother Abraham struck my brother Aaron because he said something disrespectful to a teacher. Then my father struck Aaron too. "How dare you be disrespectful to a teacher!" Aaron wasn't beaten or hurt, but it was frightening to me. I loved my brothers very much. My oldest brother Abraham was always very thoughtful and protective of his younger brothers. I remember the event precisely because it was so unusual. It had never happened before and never happened again.

Honestly, other than the tension that we felt from Polish anti-Semitism, our life in Radom was idyllic. I wish I had photographs to show how lovely life had been. But only two family photographs have survived the war. The first is a picture of my oldest brother, Abraham. He is wearing a hat that would be readily recognized in Poland as that of a university student. The picture was taken while he was attending the university in Krakow, probably in 1938. It was unusual for Jewish boys to go to university in Poland, but Abraham was unbelievably talented. He was absolutely brilliant, fluent in Polish, Yiddish, Hebrew, Russian, French, and English. At the age of eighteen, he was a freelance correspondent to *The New York Times* and *The London Times*, writing dispatches in perfect English.

Since my oldest brother was eight years my senior, I remember Abraham in the most idealistic way—tall, handsome, with blond hair and blue eyes, and the confidence of a natural leader. He was prominent in the Zionist youth groups. After graduating from the university, Abraham decided that he wanted to be a *chalutz*, which is a pioneer in Israel. At that time, Israel needed skilled laborers and craftsmen more than scholars and scientists. They needed people who could build a modern nation from an ancient desert. So, to be more useful, Abraham started training to become a locksmith or a mechanic just before the war broke out.

My oldest brother, Abraham, in his university clothes, about 1938.

The only other family picture that survived the war is of my second oldest brother, Aaron. The photograph was taken about 1938 when he was still in high school in Radom. Aaron was a year and a half younger than Abraham, and five years older than me. He was skinny and dark. He was the best math student in the whole school, and a genius in chemistry and physics. In the summer of 1939, Aaron had graduated from high school and was looking forward to attending the university in Warsaw.

Both of my oldest brothers were brilliant young men. Both were ardent Zionists, who loved to discuss Zionism and Jewish thinkers like Jabotinsky, Grossman and Greenblum. Wherever there was a debate about Jewish politics or philosophy, they were right in the middle of it. The pride I felt in watching my older brothers played a huge part in my own Jewish pride and identity, which I carry to this day.

My second oldest brother, Aaron, in high school, about 1938.

My sister Ann was three and a half years older than me. Her Jewish name was "Chana," but they called her "Andzia" in Polish. As the only girl, Ann was the darling of the family, cute, cuddly, and smart. She spent so much time with her two best friends, Marysia Tenenbaum and Hanka Leslau, that they called themselves "the Holy Trio."[3]

The youngest siblings were my brother Joseph and me. We were closest in age, about a year and a half apart, so we tended to play together the most.

As for my father, he was just great. He was a very loving parent and husband. With his sharp mind and inventiveness, my father could have achieved whatever he aspired to. As I said, he was a *voyageur* for many years, but in the years just before the war he invented a new kind of glue. Though he had no formal education in chemistry, he created a formula for glue using lime and casein, which is a protein in cheese. Father's glue was similar to what we know today as Elmer's Glue, which was originally a casein-based glue. At that time, my father's glue was a new idea in Europe that offered a better alternative. In fact, it became so successful that my father quit his traveling sales job and started a little factory. The factory was in the rear of the courtyard, right across from our apartment at Pierackiego 26. Later, after the Germans imprisoned the Jews in the Radom ghetto in early 1940, there was a short time when we were given a special permit to leave the ghetto each day to continue working in Father's glue factory.

In September, 1938, I turned thirteen years old and it was time to become a bar mitzvah. I remember my mother hired a bar mitzvah tutor. He was skinny as straw and wore shabby clothes like a beggar. He seemed very old to me, though he was probably in his twenties. Twice a week, the tutor would come to our house to give me bar mitzvah lessons and my mother would feed him. He gulped the tea and devoured the meal as if it was the only food he ever ate. The truth was that I did not need tutoring, but the poor man needed to make a living. It was another way that my mother gave *tzedekah*, charity.

When the day of my bar mitzvah came, I recited a special prayer that my father had said at his own bar mitzvah. After the Torah scrolls were returned to the Holy Ark and just before the doors are closed, I recited the words from Psalm 137, which is not part of the traditional service: *Im eshkachech Yerushalayim tishkach yehmeenee.* "If I forget you, O Jerusalem, let my right hand forget its skill, let my tongue cleave to the roof of my mouth. If I remember you not; if I set not Jerusalem above my highest joy." It is a belief that has always stayed with me.

---

[3]  Marysia described my sister and mother in her own Holocaust memoir titled *Looking Back* (by Mania Salinger, Ferne Press, 2006).

# Chapter Two

---

# The Blood Red Moon

In the summer of 1939, my family rented a cottage in the country. One evening, I was lounging outdoors and I fell asleep in the lazy summer heat. When I woke up, the moon was shining on me, full and red. A blood red moon. It scared me. It was a superstition in Poland that a red moon means that something bloody is going to happen. People said it meant that war was coming.

The threat of war was nothing new by then. My family followed current events closely, reading the newspapers and listening to the radio. We knew all about the rise of Hitler and the Nazis. We watched as Germany swallowed up Austria in the *Anschluss* of March, 1938. We watched as Hitler's army seized the Sudetenland of Czechoslovakia in October, 1938, and we grew more nervous as the Nazis launched the brutal violence of *Kristallnacht* against German Jews in November, 1938. A month later, the Germans started howling for territory in Poland. They demanded the city of Danzig and all of the land of the so-called Polish Corridor. The Poles were outraged and worried, of course. Locally, they organized a big public demonstration in Radom. My family and I went to the city plaza to show our national spirit. But the Poles rejected our support. "Go home Jews," they sneered, "this is not your problem." Even in their patriotism, the Poles hated Jews.

But nothing would satisfy Hitler's lust for an empire. In March, 1939, the German army marched into the Czechoslovakian areas of Bohemia and Moravia. After that, it seemed to most people that war was inevitable. My parents were worried. Like most Europeans, they remembered how terrible World War I had been. All through the summer of 1939, there were rumors that war was coming, along with new rumors that the Germans and the Russians were plotting to split Poland between them. But people still hoped that war would not happen.

---

"Hitler won't be fool enough to invade Poland," they said, "because France and England will come to protect us." Though I was just a boy of fourteen, I was well aware of the growing anxiety. I had heard the news about this or that German invasion, but it was hard to conceive of it happening to us in Poland. I remember listening to Hitler screaming on the radio and it scared me.

This is what was happening in the summer of 1939 when my family was on vacation in the country and I woke to the sight of the blood red moon. On the first day of September, the Germans launched their *blitzkrieg* against Poland. My family hurried home as quickly as we could. The Polish Army was stunned by the Germans' Messerschmitts and tanks. Radom itself was bombed from the very beginning because there were several factories that made military equipment for the Polish army. By September 6th, the Polish army retreated from Radom and there was panic in the city. "The Germans are coming! The Germans are coming!"

Like many other citizens of Radom, my family tried to escape the danger. We thought we would be safe if we fled east to Pulawy, the town where my grandparents lived. They lived above a grocery store in a two story building. It was located across the street from a Polish army base, at a major intersection where the road south from Warsaw intersected with the road from Radom to Lublin. Pulawy was on the eastern side of the Vistula River, and we figured the German invasion would have to stop there and the Polish army would be right across the street. So, my father hired a horse and wagon, we loaded whatever we could and fled in the middle of the night. We rode through the night and the next day, often shaken by the thump and crunch of bombs. It didn't take long to realize that there was no place to run. The German army marched into Radom on September 8th and soon overtook us on the road to Pulawy. Polish and Jewish refugees were chased from the road as the German army roared past in their trucks and tanks. We didn't need a radio to know that the Germans were crushing the Polish army. It was the same everywhere, as the final remnants of the Polish army retreated and surrendered.

The Germans crossed the River Vistula and captured Pulawy around September 14th so the German soldiers were already there before we arrived. On September 17, 1939, the Soviet Red Army launched their own invasion from the east and occupied the eastern half of Poland. Just like they had planned, Germany and Russia divided Poland between them. Poland disappeared from the map.

We stayed for a week with Grandma and Grandpa in Pulawy. But now that the Germans had conquered everything and the bombings had ceased, there was no reason to remain. So we loaded up the horse and cart and traveled back to our home in Radom. We expected to resume a somewhat normal life, but the Germans immediately began to persecute the Jews. They closed the schools for Jewish children. Every Jewish adult had to carry a work permit. At any moment, the Germans could yank anyone from the street for forced labor. Almost as soon as we had returned, some German soldiers pulled me off the street to push trucks and cars that had stalled. The Germans would force Jews to scrub and clean the streets. The Orthodox Jews were the easiest targets for abuse by the Germans. If they saw a Jew in traditional garb, they would spit on him, or tear his clothes, or cut off his beard. The Germans loved to mock the Jews and take photographs of their abuse.

Yom Kippur, the Day of Atonement, fell on September 23rd that year. Random beatings of Jews were already so common in Radom that we were apprehensive about going to synagogue. We feared that the synagogue would be a target, but it was unthinkable not to go to *shul* on the holiest of Jewish holidays. So we went. Sure enough, when the Jewish men stepped outside after services, the Germans grabbed us and forced us to clean the filthy streets while still wearing our best clothes.

Within the first weeks of occupation, the Germans also began to ration bread. Everyone had to stand in line at the bakery to receive their portion. This became a big problem because the anti-Semitic Poles would curse the Jews and drive them out of the bread lines. If German soldiers were nearby, the Poles would yell, "This is a Jew, this is a Jew." And if a Jew succeeded in reaching the front of the line, the bread was already gone. In the beginning, my oldest brother Abraham would stand in the line for our family because he could pass for Polish with his blond hair, blue eyes and university cap.

The persecution of the Jews in Radom became a little worse each day. No Jewish male of working age was safe from being beaten or suddenly kidnapped from the street and forced to do work. I remember a day when I stepped outside onto our tiny balcony over Pierackiego Street and my mother yelled at me. "Come inside, Sol, before the Germans see you!"

Given the situation, my family had a long discussion. Although it would break up our family, it was decided that my two older brothers, Abraham and Aaron, would escape to Lvov in the Russian-occupied section of Poland. They picked Lvov because my father had some friends there from his days as a traveling salesman. Many of their peers from the Zionist group *HaShomer Ha'tzair* also fled from Radom to the Russian-occupied zone at that time.

I remember the day my two brothers were packed to go. "Goodbye boys, we hope to see you soon," my parents said. "Don't worry. England and France will beat the Germans in a month or two, and Poland will be free again."

They believed it. Everyone believed it. France and England were considered the strongest countries in the world. We expected the Germans to retreat back to Germany with their tails between their legs. We never imagined that the Germans could defeat the whole world, and we never imagined that this would be the last time we saw Abraham and Aaron alive.

My older brothers made it safely to the large city of Lvov about 200 miles to the southeast. Then, they moved to a small village outside of the city, where my brothers took jobs teaching Hebrew to Jewish children. They were safe, for the time being.

Meanwhile, the rest of us tried to make the best of things in Radom. Although I was only 14 years old, my youth was no protection from forced labor. When the first snow fell in October, some German soldiers grabbed me from the sidewalk and forced me to shovel snow from the streets. Another time I was forced to clean horse stables. Another time my brother Joseph and I were forcibly taken all the way to Lublin to chop wood for a day. There were many such instances. The Germans would grab Jews for forced labor anytime they wanted—to sweep the street, or push vehicles, or shovel snow, whatever they wanted. "For the Fuehrer, for the Fuehrer," the German soldiers would bellow. When the cars and trucks would not start in the winter cold, they would shout, "*Juden, Juden, Auto schieben!*" ("Jews, Jews, push the car!"), beating anyone within arm's length. You could not walk on the sidewalk, but had to walk in the gutter, and if you saw a German coming, you had to tip your hat in respect—or else.

I think it was November, 1939, when the Germans ordered every Jew in Radom to wear a yellow arm band with the Star of David and the word *Jude*—Jew. The yellow star was meant to be a mark of shame. The Germans considered the Jews to be nothing but cockroaches. Each day seemed to bring new restrictions. Jews couldn't do this, Jews couldn't do that. Jews were forbidden to walk on the main streets. Jews could not ride on public transportation. The Germans seized Jewish properties and businesses, including my father's little glue factory, which they gave to some German or Pole. We could do nothing to stop it.

One day we were forced to make space in our apartment for a German. He moved into one of the three bedrooms and the rest of us squeezed into the remaining two rooms. We tried to reassure ourselves that, "Well, the Germans won't be here forever."

For the first year of the German occupation, we continued to live in our apartment on Pierackiego Street. Life was hard, but not terrible yet. The biggest problem was that my father, being an able-bodied Jewish man, was in constant danger of being kidnapped by the Germans for forced labor. He might even be sent away to a work camp. Eventually, it was decided that my father should also escape to Lvov and join my brothers in the Russian zone. We knew from letters that Abraham and Aaron were safe, and life was definitely better for Jews there.

Of course, my mother was afraid to be left alone with three children in an uncertain world, but it seemed like a wise move. Our family was not unique. There were thousands of other Jewish families who packed up and fled east to the Russian zone of Poland. Unfortunately, Stalin did not like having the Jews there either. So, in 1940, he deported about 200,000 Polish Jews to labor settlements in Siberia and the former Soviet states of Tajikistan and Uzbekistan in Central Asia. Although cruel at the time, Stalin's deportations ultimately saved the largest group of Polish Jews from death in the Holocaust. Naturally, we knew nothing of this at the time. We only knew how much we missed Abraham, Aaron and Father.

In the winter of 1940, the Germans ordered the creation of the Radom ghetto as a prison for the Jews. They actually built two Radom ghettos. The "Big Ghetto" was created in the old quarter of the city and held about 27,000 Jews. The small ghetto was built in the suburb of Glinice and held about 5,000 Jews. By March, 1941, the ghetto prisons were ready. Every Jew in Radom was ordered into the ghetto. We said goodbye to our apartment and comfortable furniture. We saved a few personal belongings and crowded into a single room in the Big Ghetto, where we lived together for the next year. Once we had been comfortably middle class. The ghetto was the great equalizer. Now everybody was dirt poor.

The ghetto was locked on April 7, 1941. To keep our hopes up, we organized a Zionist youth club. Even in the ghetto, we dreamed of Israel and Zionism. It was absolutely forbidden for Jews to congregate or break curfew, but we were willing to risk getting shot for the chance to sing our Hebrew songs and dance. In fact, our secret meeting place had a little patch of green—a sort of garden in the ghetto. So we called our group *"Gan"*, the Hebrew word for garden. There were twenty or thirty of us, boys and girls, who gathered around the fire to sing the same Zionist songs over and over. We sang the ancient oath from the Babylonian exile—*Im eshkachech Yerushalayim*—never forget Jerusalem.

The *Gan* also published a secret record of our activities. Sometimes we had visitors from the Zionist underground movement, mostly the *HaShomer Ha'tzair*. One speaker was an elderly man who had been on vacation from Israel when the war started. He was caught by the Germans and not allowed to return home. We listened with wide eyes as he told us about life in the Promised Land.

In the beginning of the Radom ghetto, there was no organized work to speak of. Most people lived on whatever savings they had and bought food and items on the black market. The Germans would frequently round up Jews from the ghetto for forced labor assignments. No one could refuse to work. The Germans would give the laborers a little soup for a day of labor. That was how the Jews survived in the ghetto from day to day. My brother and I were different. We had work permits that allowed us to leave the ghetto to go to work in my father's glue factory. A Jewish policeman escorted us to and from work because we were not allowed to walk alone in the Gentile section.

After our family was locked in the Radom ghetto, my mother started trying to get my father back from the city of Lvov and my brothers back from the little village outside Lvov. She decided that whatever will happen, it should happen to all of us together. But the Germans put an end to that hope. On June 22, 1941, the German Army suddenly launched their *blitzkrieg* against the Soviet Union. Just like every country before, the German Army crushed the Russians and they raced across Poland and on through Russia itself. By July 2nd, the German Army had captured the city of Lvov. Almost immediately, the German SS and their new anti-Semitic allies, the Ukrainian nationalists, began slaughtering the Jews living in the region. By July 3rd, they had already murdered 4,000 Jews in and around Lvov. Then, on July 25th, the Ukrainians unleashed a three day pogrom that massacred another 2,000 Jews in the Lvov area.

At the time, we knew nothing of these events. We never heard from my brothers again, and we never learned what happened to Abraham and Aaron until many years later. About ten years after the war, I met a man who was in the same village outside of Lvov at the time of these pogroms. He remembered the two Finkelstein brothers from Radom who were working as teachers in the village. The man heard that my poor brothers were beaten to death with clubs and shovels by a Ukrainian mob. My dear brothers Abraham and Aaron were murdered for no reason except for being Jewish. Two beautiful souls were lost. It is a pain I feel even today, almost 70 years later.

Having no information about my brothers and my father from the war zone was worrisome, but we did our best to go on living in our tiny ghetto room. We knew that my grandparents from Pulawy had been deported to Treblinka, but we could not accept they had been murdered along with tens of thousands of other innocent Jews.

We also heard very discouraging news of overwhelming German victories in Russia. We could see the proof of German power with our own eyes as they marched thousands and thousands of Russian prisoners through the city. They trudged past us, dressed in rags, looking more like animals than human beings, begging for water. But if we offered any help, the Germans beat us. The sight of those wretched Russian soldiers destroyed our hopes that Hitler could be defeated. The Germans seemed invincible.

As the winter of 1941-1942 passed, my brother and I continued to be escorted each day to work in Father's former glue factory. But then the Germans revoked our permits to leave the ghetto and we had no work. In the spring of 1942, the Germans began to deport the leaders of the Jewish community in Radom ghetto. This started persistent rumors that the Nazis were going to liquidate the entire ghetto. People became desperate to get jobs that could help protect them and their families from deportation. The best jobs were in the munitions factories and the automotive workshops.

My brother and I were first in our family to get work permits. By claiming to be mechanics, we obtained jobs working for the German Air Force, the *Luftwaffe*, which had a garage just outside and against the wall of the ghetto. The closest I ever came to being a mechanic was I knew which end of the screwdriver to hold. Without knowing it, my brother and I were already doing two things that increased one's chances of survival during the war. First, seize any opportunity that can improve your condition, and second, stay close to someone you can trust so that you can protect and help each other.

My mother and sister Ann were next to get work permits. They did housecleaning work for a shop run by the German army, the *Wehrmacht*. Working directly for the Germans was considered the best way to keep safe. Ann later persuaded the Germans to give jobs to her two best friends, too. The "Holy Trio" of Ann, Marysia and Hanka worked together doing various jobs outside the ghetto, like washing windows, making beds and cleaning offices. Ultimately, they gained desk jobs in the *Wehrmacht* office because they could all speak German quite well. Their boss was a kind middle-aged German officer named Baker.

On August 5, 1942, the Nazis suddenly struck. In a single day, they liquidated the entire Glinice ghetto. The SS surrounded the smaller of the two Radom ghettos and, at midnight, the Jewish policemen drove all the people from their apartments. Those who tried to hide were shot on the spot. The SS assembled the Jews and picked out the ones with work permits, about 800, who were sent to the big Radom ghetto. Then the SS shot about 600 old people and children and deported everyone else, about 6,000 Jews, including 2,000 from the large ghetto, to be gassed at their new extermination camp at Treblinka. We were in the big ghetto, but I remember that horrible night because we were locked in and warned to not go out. There were shouts, gunshots, screams and barking dogs. My poor uncle Josef, his wife and their two lovely children were deported that night, as well as my sister Ann's dear friend Hanka and her mother.

After the Germans liquidated the smaller Glinice ghetto, everyone was afraid—for good reason—because the Germans soon came back to wipe out the big ghetto. Between midnight August 16 and August 18, 1942, the SS forced 20,000 more Jewish men, women and children into cattle cars to be gassed at Treblinka.

My mother and sister Ann were saved by the actions of their kind German boss, Herr Baker. When Baker learned the date of the next deportation, he ordered his workers to return to the Radom ghetto to pack their clothes and valuables and return to work immediately. But Ann's best friend Marysia failed to return to the office. Ann acted quickly. She gave her watch to one of the German guards as a bribe to go to Marysia's apartment in the ghetto and bring her back before the liquidation began. Ann, my mother, Marysia and about thirty women and girls stayed overnight in an empty warehouse, while Mr. Baker stood guard outside with a shotgun. They could hear gunshots and screams during that long terrible night. My sister Ann had saved her friend Marysia's life, but her Holy Trio was finished—Hanka was gassed at Treblinka.

At the same time, my brother and I were saved by the *Luftwaffe* soldiers who didn't want to lose their free workers. They also knew that the Nazis were about to exterminate the Radom ghetto, so they told us to stay overnight in the garage next to the ghetto and not return to our room. We tried to sleep in some cars that night, but the sounds from the other side of the ghetto wall were too horrible. In his brief unpublished memoir, my brother Joseph wrote this description of what happened that long night:

> "All night there was movement of people. All night there were cries and calling of names—Camale, Shigruele, Yosale—all children's names. The parents tried not to let loose of their children. All night there was shooting and more shooting. At daybreak, a deafening silence surrounded the ghetto. No sign of life. It was horrifying. At about 7 a.m., our keepers lined us up, about eight in all and marched us before the Germans . . . . They checked our papers. They were in order with the exception of the only girl in our group, who worked as a maid. They marched her away from us about ten feet. Bang—she was not amongst us any more. I still shiver at the thought. We passed many corpses. However, to this corpse, we were immediate witnesses . . . ."

The SS had now reduced Radom ghetto to a tenth of its original size. Of the 2,000 Jews remaining in the ghetto, nearly everyone worked for the German Army or Air Force. After the mass deportations, people were desperate for jobs outside the ghetto because they believed it might offer better protection from future deportation. My mother and sister were fortunate in gaining jobs at a work-farm outside and north of Radom, in the small village of Wsola. There were about one hundred male and female workers who walked four miles each day from the ghetto to the Wsola work-farm. After a while, the Germans erected a barrack so the workers would not lose so much time marching back and forth from the ghetto. The Wsola farm turned out to be a decent labor camp without brutality.

At about the same time, my brother Joe and I were assigned to work at a munitions factory in Radom, which had about 500 workers. It was short-lived. Only a week later, I was suddenly seized from the ghetto street by the SS Commandant, the *Unterscharführer*, who was looking for a car mechanic. I tried to talk the Commandant out of the idea. "Yes, sir, I'm a mechanic, but I work for the *Luftwaffe.*"

"You're not working for the *Luftwaffe* anymore," he snorted. "You're working for me. You'll be my personal mechanic."

Just like that, I was torn from my brother, the final connection to my family. I was sixteen years old and it was my first time alone. I was terrified. Joe remained in Radom ghetto while I was taken to a nearby labor camp. There, I was given the job of caring for the personal automobile of the SS Commandant. He owned a little Fiat and my job was to wash it and change the oil. I didn't know anything about cars, but luckily someone showed me a few things. For a few months, my position was not so bad. I worked alone in the garage. I was given adequate food. I had blankets, which I used to make myself a bed on the floor.

During the time I was working at the garage, my mother was determined to reunite our family. Using persuasion and bribes, she succeeded in getting my brother Joseph transferred from the Radom ghetto to the Wsola work-farm. Joe was safer now, but my situation soon became perilous.

A *kapo*, a Jewish prisoner who supervised other prisoners, who was a friend of my brother, suddenly ran into the garage one day. "Sol, you have to run away!" he warned me. "Listen, someone was caught stealing gasoline from the garage. He told the Germans that he bought it from the little Jew boy in the garage. Sol, you know what happens. They're going to shoot you tomorrow morning at 11. You have to escape and save yourself!"

My stomach clenched and I felt the blood run from my face. This was a death sentence. With the Germans, there would be no chance of a trial, no explanations to prove my innocence. The truth was that two Poles had been smuggling the stolen gas. But the truth did not matter. I would be executed in the morning. There was nothing I could do but send word of the bad news to my family at the work-farm. At least, they would know what happened to me. It was sad to wait alone in the garage. Not many people will ever know what it is like to be a 16 year-old boy, all alone, counting the hours to your certain death.

While I waited for my execution, my sister Ann, who had received the message that I was to be executed, went straight to the German in command of Wsola. He was a major in the regular German army, and had contempt for the Nazis and their brutality. Not all Germans were bad. Some were kind and respectful like the Major and Herr Baker. At first, the Major said he could do nothing. But Ann was a clever 19 year-old and very brave. "You have a car, sir," she persisted. "My brother is a wonderful car mechanic. He could fix your car." It worked. The Major wrote a transfer order to the SS saying that he needed me specifically to repair his car and immediately dispatched one of his lieutenants in his personal car to come get me.

It was about 10:30 in the morning and I was counting the minutes to my execution. Someone called my name. I stood and walked outside the garage, expecting to meet a firing squad. Instead, it was a bright, beautiful morning and there was only this German lieutenant. He escorted me outside the gate to the Major's car.

Minutes later, as I left the camp in safety, I heard the gunshots that were meant for me. In the cruel logic of Nazi justice, someone had to die as an example to the others. Since I was gone, the SS guards chose another Jewish prisoner at random and promptly murdered him. Through quick thinking, courage and determination, my sister Ann saved my life.

# CHAPTER THREE

## Descending

After my miraculous escape from death, I was once more reunited with my mother, sister and brother on the forced labor work-farm at Wsola. We all lived together as a family in an open wooden barrack, which we shared with four or five other families, divided by curtains. Each family had their own living area and a tiny little stove and we shared a communal bathroom. Everyone worked from dawn to dusk. My brother had somehow learned enough to become the camp electrician. I cleaned the stables and did manual labor. My mother and sister were working in the fields, weeding, hoeing, or picking the crops.

All in all, after the experience in the Radom ghetto, life on the Wsola work-farm was not so bad. We could move about freely and the Germans did not mistreat us. They gave us enough potatoes, bread and vegetables to eat, and if we needed something extra, we could barter with the local Polish farmers, using whatever valuables we had left from before the war. It seems odd to say, but these were good Germans. They were in the regular army, not the SS, and treated us more like employees than slaves. The Germans even trusted me to clean their firearms! One of my jobs was to take their pistols and rifles, break them apart, oil and clean the parts, and reassemble them. It never dawned on me to use the weapons against the Germans.

We settled into our work routines and hoped the war would someday end. As the fourth year of the war began in the fall of 1942, I turned 17, and it looked like nothing could stop Hitler. Earlier that summer, we could see waves of German planes, tanks and trucks moving eastward toward the Russian front. They had so much military power and it seemed never-ending. This turned out to be the build-up to another massive German offensive against the Russians. For many months, there was news of German victory after German victory after

German victory. At Wsola, we would get war news from the Polish peasants, or by finding a page from an old Polish newspaper. We even listened to a secret radio, which was absolutely forbidden on penalty of death. The Germans were very good about boasting about their victories—and there were plenty.

Meanwhile, my mother finally heard news that my father was still alive in Lvov. She paid a huge amount of money to bribe a SS man to travel to Lvov (which was now renamed Lemberg by the Germans) and bring him back to us. My brother Joe also helped by giving money and his leather coat to bribe the SS man. The SS man found our father and brought him back by train to the work-farm in Wsola. It was a wonderful reunion. This was probably in July, 1942, and we had not seen Father for nearly two years. He was so happy to see his children again, especially me. As the youngest child, I was his favorite son. What joy to have our father back!

My father convinced the Germans at Wsola that he was a *tischler*, a carpenter. He probably knew as much about carpentry as my brother knew about electricity or I knew about car mechanics—nothing. But my father was smart and learned quickly. In fact, he built a fabulous greenhouse from random scraps of wood, which impressed the Germans so much that they liked to show it off to visitors. As I said, these were decent Germans, regular *Wehrmacht* soldiers, not the SS, so they were very respectful to my father. In comparison to other ghettos and forced labor camps, Wsola was almost pleasant. During our time at Wsola, there was only occasional tension in the camp, such as when a Polish partisan in the area had killed a German soldier, or when some Jews were being hunted in the woods. When this happened, the Germans would become more cautious and locked the barracks at night. But nothing terrible happened to anyone.

I also remember a Jewish woman who arrived one day at the Wsola farm. She had somehow escaped from the Nazi extermination camp at Treblinka. She told us terrible stories of how the Nazis were gassing thousands of Jews every day. No one believed her. Everyone thought she was insane. Poison gas? Mass murder? Who could imagine human beings doing something so horrible? We named the girl "Treblinka" and made fun of her.

Suddenly, one day in December, 1942, several trucks arrived at the Wsola farm. The Germans loaded everyone up and moved us to another forced labor camp in a little town called Pionki about 20 miles to the east. Pionki was the site of a large munitions factory that was hidden in a thick forest. At the time of our arrival, Pionki was still a forced labor camp with several hundred workers in civilian clothes. It was guarded by Ukrainians and operated by a reasonably kind German businessman named Herr Brendt. Men and women were housed in separate barracks near the factory, but there were no fences or barriers to prevent people from mixing and talking. Our family was still able to be together.

The Pionki munitions factory was a very large operation. It is too complicated to explain because there are many different steps to making gun powder. The prisoners in one shop would prepare the cotton; the next shop would soak the cotton in acid and alcohol; the next would boil it in tubs; the next would dry it and add more alcohol; the next would dry it again; and finally, the last shop would blend the different batches of dried gunpowder. Each member of my family had a different job in the assembly line. My sister's job was to saturate the cotton in alcohol and chemicals to make it combustive. My father worked in the drying division. I worked in the blending division. All of this work was quite dangerous because the materials could easily catch fire or explode—and sometimes there were fires and accidents.

Everyone worked twelve hours a day, every day. My mother and my brother Joe had jobs outside the munitions factory. My mother stayed in camp as a kitchen laborer. My brother said he was a mechanic, so they put him in charge of maintaining the water pump. He had the easiest job because all he had to do was sit by the pump to make sure it was running.

Every morning at 6 a.m., the Ukrainian guards would line us up outside the barracks and march us to the munitions factory. The Ukrainians despised Jews and were very cruel, often more cruel than the Nazis. It was their fun to kick a prisoner to death. The Ukrainians forced us to sing happy songs while we marched. It was their big joke. If anyone did not sing loud enough and pretend that he was happy, the Ukrainian guards would beat him. Since I was young, I was always in the front line. To this day I remember some of the profane Ukrainian songs that we were forced to sing as we marched.

But there was at least one day that we sang for our own joy. There was an entertainer in the camp with blond hair whom we called the "Gayleh Meyer." Gayleh means yellow, and Meyer was his name. We sat in the grass as he performed songs and told wonderful stories. It was a rare opportunity to remember the simple pleasures of life, a moment of joy that enabled us to forget our growling stomachs and grim existence.

In the spring of 1943, we heard the news of the Warsaw ghetto uprising, which began on the first night of Passover on April 19, 1943. For the first time, Jews dared to fight back with weapons. And, for the first time, the Germans were apprehensive because they thought rebellion might spread across the other ghettos and forced labor camps. We were less than 60 miles from Warsaw. The eight days of Passover were nearly over by the time we heard the exciting news. There were many rumors, but the only thing we knew for certain was that the rebellion had happened.

We could see a clear change of attitude in the Germans after the Warsaw uprising. I believe that this was also around the time that the SS took direct command of the Pionki labor camp and turned it into a concentration camp.

Until then, we had worked in our own civilian clothes, which were marked to identify us as prisoners. But the SS issued striped uniforms and the rules and punishments became much harsher. I remember an execution in which the SS hanged three Russian prisoners who had tried to escape. The SS and Ukrainians gathered all the prisoners in a circle and forced us to watch the hanging. The Germans were drinking beer and whiskey, laughing out loud, and making jokes like it was a party. They kept laughing, pointing to the hanging bodies, saying, "Look, look, look."

Of all the brutal things I saw at Pionki, there was one horrible incident that haunts me to this day. Five Jewish boys escaped from camp by cutting a hole in the fence and were caught the next morning. It was two brothers from Kielce and three other boys from the town of Skarzysko. The SS summoned all the prisoners from their work details and lined us up in an open courtyard with a gallows in the center. The SS had their barking dogs and yelled at us to stand at attention and watch the execution. The hangman was a Jewish prisoner. The Germans had gotten him drunk on beer and bribed him with promises of bread. As the soldiers marched the five young prisoners to the gallows, I recognized the two brothers from Kielce because I worked with them in the factory. Then the young man standing beside me suddenly gasped out loud. "Oh my God, they are my brothers!" he whispered. The poor man had to watch his two brothers mount the gallows. My heart ached as the Jewish hangman slipped a noose around the neck of each boy. It was sickening as the boys dropped down and the ropes strangled the life from them. Five deaths might seem insignificant among the millions of people killed by the Nazis, but not when they are boys, and not when you know them, and not when you are watching from up close. It is a terrible, terrible sight.

As the months passed into the fall and winter of 1943, we began to hear encouraging rumors that the Russians were driving the Germans back. The spring of 1944 brought even more good news of German defeats. The Russians were pushing the Germans back and back, steadily driving them westward into Poland and the Ukraine. By July, 1944, the Russians had reached Warsaw and the Vistula River, only 60 miles away. We could hear the rumbling of the heavy artillery and our spirits soared. "Here come the Russians! It won't be long now. We'll be liberated."

Then disaster struck. While working on an artesian well, a heavy metal pipe fell on my brother's foot, breaking his ankle. The Jewish foremen refused to send Joseph to the hospital because they knew that an injury like that was a sure death sentence. Instead, they secretly fashioned a crude cast to support his ankle and then concealed it with a rag.

Just a week later, our hopes of liberation by the advancing Russian army were crushed. The Germans evacuated the entire Pionki concentration camp.

About 3,000 Jews were stuffed into a long line of cattle cars. The guards said they were moving us to a similar munitions plant in Czestochowa about 135 miles to the west. We traveled for three days. The cattle cars were crowded and hot, without food, water or toilets. The thirst was maddening. At one point, when the train was stopped at a railroad station, I broke through a board in the side of the cattle car and squeezed out. I was certain to be shot, but I was too desperate to care. I ran to the well, filled several canteens with water, and climbed back into the boxcar. My family drank first, then we shared the precious water with the others. With so many thirsty people, the water was limited, maybe one swallow each, but it was worth risking my life.

Then the train started to roll again. Our family huddled together, wondering what would happen next, never imagining that we were about to enter hell itself.

# Chapter Four

## Dante's Inferno

The train finally crawled to a final stop. After three long days of desperate thirst and endless waiting, the doors suddenly burst open and everything was rushed, rushed, rushed. Men were yelling and cursing, dogs were barking, the *kapos* were driving the people as soon as their feet touched the ground. They herded the men and older boys into one big group; women and small children into another. My father, brother and I went one way; my mother and sister went another; and we quickly lost sight of each other. We would have no idea of their fate until after liberation, ten months later.

At first we were stunned by the great noise and confusion, but we quickly realized that this was an extermination camp. Auschwitz. It was a gigantic complex with rows and rows of long barracks extending as far as we could see on the flat land. One sight rose above the rest: the tall chimneys of the crematorium. We had heard the horror stories. Here was the proof. As I jumped down from the cattle car, I was certain we were going to the gas chambers.

Behind me, there was a girl who was too weak to get out of the cattle car. She had once been a beauty, tall and dark-haired, so lovely that people would stop just to look at her. But now she was thin and pale, sick from cancer, and exhausted by three days of starvation and thirst in the hot cattle car. As the *kapos* barked, her boyfriend carefully lifted her onto his back and carried her. They directed him straight to the gas chambers. I can still picture that good man carrying his love to their mutual death at Auschwitz.

The *kapos* were screaming at us, driving us forward, striking people at random with their clubs—in the head, on the back, in the balls—rushing us through the selection procedure. Blood was dripping from people's heads. The weak and the old were immediately sent to the left to the gas chambers. There was one very old man who could barely walk, yet the *kapos* were forcing him to run. He stumbled, fell, and fell again, and they beat him mercilessly. He, too, went straight to the gas chambers.

Meanwhile, my father, brother Joe and I proceeded with one line of men. Suddenly a voice called to my father. It was Moshe Eiger, an accountant who had worked for my father before the war. Having survived more than a year at Auschwitz, he had worked himself into an important administrative position as an "elder" in the camp. "*Yankel,*" he said in Yiddish, "*Ve yaka by doon?*" "Jakob, what are you doing over there?"

"*Ich bin mit der kinder zun,*" my father replied. "I am here with my children." Eiger said, "Come over to this line. They will kill you if you are in that line." We were in the wrong line, the line of men selected to go to the gas chambers.

So my father and I crossed over and got in the other. Then my brother Joe did the same, and was followed by Yurik Neuman, one of his friends from high school, who had heard the conversation.

We and the rest of the Pionki men and boys in this line, there must have been a thousand, were next driven into a huge, one-story brick building inside the concentration camp. Step by step, in rapid order, we were stripped of our clothes, shaved of every bit of hair, sent through the showers, and powdered with insecticide to kill lice. At every stage, there were *kapos* sitting or standing, ready to strike out with their clubs to keep us moving, always rushing us to the next step. "Go go go—go go go—go go go."

One room had about twenty prisoners with tattoo pens. We waited in twenty lines as these *screibers* rapidly tattooed a number onto the left forearm of each prisoner.

The tattooing was done in seconds, b-b-b-b-buh, b-b-b-b-buh, using a pen to mark each person's left forearm. My father was first, B-252. Then Yurik, B-253. Joseph, B-254. And me, B-255. There were a thousand of us and everyone was tattooed in maybe ten minutes. We felt some relief at this point because we knew the Germans would not bother numbering us if we were going to be gassed. Meanwhile, somewhere else in that huge concentration camp, my mother and sister Ann were going through the same process. My mother was tattooed with the number A-14546, Ann was tattooed as well.

We now know that we arrived at Auschwitz on Monday, July 31, 1944. The log records at Auschwitz verify that about 3,000 prisoners arrived that day on a train transport from the Pionki concentration camp. The men were tattooed with the numbers B-1 to B-1147, and the women were numbers A-14394 to A-15210. A total of 1,147 men and 817 women were selected for slave labor from the Pionki group, while all the others, about a thousand people, were immediately murdered in the gas chambers. Years later we learned a possible reason why many of the Pionki group had been saved. Herr Baker, the kind German boss who had protected my sister and mother from deportation from the Radom ghetto, had remained in communication with Herr Brendt, the German in charge of the Pionki camp. When Baker learned that the SS were planning to send us to Auschwitz, he may have used his influence to get a promise to reassign the Pionki munitions workers to new jobs in munitions at Auschwitz.

After receiving our tattoo numbers, the *kapos* issued striped uniforms and wooden clogs. There was no attention given to size. Pants and shirts did not match. Tall men had small pants, small men had big pants. It was up to the prisoners to trade among themselves to find uniforms that fit. Then they threw us into a barrack in one of the large divisions of Auschwitz called "Auschwitz I" for a period of quarantine. We stayed there for several days and then there was another "selection." The *kapos* lined us up to parade past the infamous Dr. Mengele. We had to remove our shirts and drop our pants so that Mengele could see us naked and determine who was too sick or weak to work. As we approached Dr. Mengele, we stood as straight and strong as possible. We feared that my brother Joseph was sure to be rejected because of his injured ankle. As luck would have it, when we dropped our pants, Joe's pants covered the cast on his ankle. Dr. Mengele then ordered everyone to run. My father and I pulled up our pant legs, but Joe did not, and we ran together. My father and I carried Joe between us, supporting him by each arm as he hobbled on his broken ankle. Since we were mixed with the crowd, the Nazis never noticed. Miraculously, Joe survived the selection. Others did not. A sad group of ten emaciated men remained behind, doomed to die in the gas chamber.

After the selection, our group was given some food, loaded into cattle cars and sent to a subcamp of Auschwitz about twenty miles away called "Sosnowiec II." It was one of two subcamps in the town of Sosnowiec (or Sosnowitz in German) and had about 850 prisoners. This camp had a small steel mill that cast the barrels for anti-aircraft cannon and artillery shells. Since I claimed to be a mechanic, I was given the job of filing a ridge of metal from each cannon barrel so that another rod would slide smoothly into the barrel. I did a terrible job. I figured I could help defeat the Germans by ruining their artillery. And I got away with it because the civilian German supervisor allowed my sloppy work to pass inspection. I think he was afraid that he himself would be accused of sabotage, or maybe he just liked me a lot. He was impressed that I spoke fluent German. In fact, I could recite Goethe better than he could.

"How did you learn to speak German so well?" he asked.

"I learned German in school."

Meanwhile, my brother Joe was given the job of sweeping the metal scrapings from the floor. I switched jobs with him so that he would not have to walk on his broken ankle. The German guards did not seem to notice. A number is a number, a face is a face. Later, though, when they realized that my brother was unable to walk, a few good Germans protected him by giving him a sit-down job in the inspection area. This was another example of Germans who were decent and kind.

My father was given the job as carpenter and usually stayed in the camp. But there were many times that he was ordered to work in the melting furnaces in the steel mill. One of the cruel guards had it in for Father. The furnace to which he was assigned by this guard looked like a scene from Dante's *Inferno*: huge hellish fires blazed under giant vats of molten steel. My father had to stand in that vicious raging heat, moving the molten steel from the oven, then pouring the red hot liquid metal into the mold. It was horrible, dangerous work and my father suffered greatly. Even today I have nightmares where I see the silhouette of my poor father struggling in front of that blazing fire like a tortured soul in Dante's *Inferno*.

In September, 1944, the war entered its sixth year, and I turned nineteen. The three of us worked at the Sosnowiec II factory from late August until mid-January 1945. During that time I befriended a Polish girl, who operated a big overhead crane. She was impressed that I could speak perfect Polish and perfect German. Our friendship rarely became closer than twenty feet because she was high up in her crane, but we somehow managed to converse. One day, I told her that we were hungry and needed bread.

"Bring me something I can sell," she said in Polish, "and I'll buy you some food."

Since I knew someone who worked in the camp laundry, I came up with the idea of selling her some stolen linen. The next day I delivered the linen to the Polish girl. She sold it, and then she brought me three loaves of bread, which I shared with my father and brother. This procedure worked so well that we did it again, and once more. But, as luck would have it, on the fourth attempt, I stole the personal linen of the Camp Commandant himself. The Polish girl was caught and betrayed me. The German guards took me directly from the factory to the concentration camp and brought me into the Commandant's office.

"Did you steal the linen?" he asked.

"Yes," I confessed.

"Why did you do it?"

"I was hungry."

"Didn't you know it was mine?"

"No, I didn't know," I said, which was the truth. "I just took some linen and sold it for three loaves of bread."

The Commandant looked at me and said, "Jew, I'll give you a choice: you can be shot or you can be hanged."

"If I have a choice," I answered, "I choose life."

The Commandant smiled. He was greatly amused that a Jewish boy, 19 years old, would dare to answer an SS officer and the Commandant of an Auschwitz subcamp so boldly, and could do it in perfect German.

Just then, the telephone rang on the other side of a partition and one of his adjutants entered. He approached the Commandant to whisper something to him. Then the Commandant picked up his own telephone and answered. I watched as his expression fell and blood drained from his face. He was visibly shaken as he hung up the telephone.

"Go back to your barracks," he said, "I'll get to you later."

Since my father worked in the camp, he was there when I returned to our barrack. He was surprised to see me. "Sol, what are you doing here?"

I explained how I had stolen the linen that belonged to the Commandant and now I was going to be executed. A moment later, we heard the camp bell announcing a *Blocksperrung*, a lock down. It was standard procedure to recall the factory workers to the camp, have a lockdown, and then assemble all the prisoners to make them watch a punishment or execution. The prisoners would be forced to stand in neat formations and watch as the victim would be beaten, hanged or shot. When my brother Joe returned with the other workers, he was upset to discover that I was the one who was about to be executed. "This is it, I am going to die," I said grimly, then kissed my father and brother in a final farewell. It was the second time the Nazis had specifically ordered my execution. We waited.

It might seem odd, but I was not distraught over my death sentence. After six years of forced labor, hunger and misery, our lives were not worth much. We were just existing, enduring a life without joy or meaning. When the Commandant appeared in the assembly yard, I was expecting to be pulled out of the formation and shot. Instead he announced, "We have orders to move the camp because the Russian Army is coming. Everyone will get some food and a blanket for the march." Now I understood the phone call and why the Commandant's face had turned pale. In the haste and confusion of evacuating the camp, my death sentence and execution were overlooked. Once again, God stepped in to save me from execution—and He used a million Russian soldiers to do it!

# CHAPTER FIVE

## Death March to Mauthausen

The date of the death march, I have since learned, was January 17, 1945. As we began the march, no one could have imagined the horror that lay ahead. It would be two grueling weeks of marching through snow and frost, without food, water or overcoats, trudging barefoot in wooden clogs. The bread that we were given at the start of the march was gone in three days. The march was slow and agonizing. We marched about 30 miles until we came to the Auschwitz subcamps at Gleiwitz (or Glinice in Polish). There, our group of 800 from Sosnowiec II was joined by over a thousand more prisoners from some other subcamps, all being evacuated before the Russian advance. We could hear cannons and gunfire and, at one point, the Russian army was just a half mile away. We could actually see them! The German commander was willing to let us go free. "Let's just leave them," he said to his subordinates, "the Russians are here."

We were so close to liberation, but a couple of fanatical SS officers threatened the commander. "We'll tell the Gestapo that you let the Jews go. We have an order to take them to Austria and we will take them to Austria." The commander gave in to their threat and the death march continued. At that time, there were 95% of us alive who had started from Sosnowiec II.

When it was clear that the Germans were not going to let us go, a number of prisoners tried to hide in piles of straw and others attempted to run toward the Russians. The SS shot the prisoners who hid and easily gunned down those who ran, then drove the rest of us faster to escape from the approaching Russian army.

There were about 2,000 prisoners as we resumed the march. We marched continuously, night and day. In fact, the SS would often use the night to march us through towns and thereby conceal the evidence of their brutality and defeat.

Occasionally, the march would pause for two or three hours and everyone would collapse on the cold open ground to sleep or rest. We would scoop snow for water and to stave off the pangs of starvation. We had some blankets because they gave us blankets at the start of the march. We would try to cover each other as we rested, but a wet blanket is no protection against frost.

Then, the Germans would order us to stand up and start marching once more. If someone could not get up, they would be shot. If anyone stopped for any reason, they would be shot. If someone collapsed, a soldier would walk over and put a rifle to his head. The pop of a rifle was a common sound. The dead were left where they died. Walk, walk, walk, walk, then "pop," another man dead. Walk, walk, walk, walk, then "pop," another man dead. The death march is impossible for sane people to imagine. Starving, frozen, without food or water or coats or sleep, people were dropping dead and being shot right in front of your eyes. But you could not help them. You had to walk past them without a glance because if you stopped or looked, you were liable to be shot by the SS.

As we slogged across the frozen land, we encountered hundreds of Hungarian and German civilians fleeing from Hungary to escape the Russians. These were Hitler's *Volksdeutsche*, Germans who had moved into the conquered territories to take over farms and businesses and now feared retribution for their years of abuse. The roads were clogged with horse-drawn carts and wagons, piled high with their possessions.

As the march went on, men were driven to greater desperation by starvation. There was no food or water, other than eating snow or finding some scrap frozen in the field. Some dared to try to steal food from the Hungarian and German refugee wagons. Once my brother Joe was able to get close to one of the wagons and stole a loaf of bread! But as soon as the other prisoners saw that Joe had food, they jumped on him, tearing at the bread, ripping pieces away until he had nothing but a morsel squeezed in each fist. Joe shared the two pieces of bread with Father and me—a tiny godsend.

I had better luck than Joe. One day I managed to steal a long piece of brown soap from a passing wagon, which I offered to a German soldier. He could have shot me, but he knew the war was lost. He traded me a loaf of bread, which I shared with my brother and Father. I still remember how fabulous that bread tasted.

We slogged on through the bitter January cold, leaving a trail of dead along the road. In a situation like that, your mind shuts down in the same way that your body goes numb from the cold. Your legs somehow move, but you don't control them. There was no talking as we marched, no words of encouragement. Just tramping, tramping, tramping. My brother and I positioned our father between us, supporting him because he had become very, very weak. The only thing I remember is that Father kept saying, "We've got to survive to avenge. We've got to survive to avenge." He said that every morning and every night. "We've got to survive to avenge."

I think the death march finally ended at a railroad station in a town called Wodzislaw (Loslau in German) around the last day of January, 1945. There they loaded us into open coal cars for a windy, freezing ride to Mauthausen concentration camp. It took about a day for the coal cars to reach Mauthausen, which is just outside of Linz in the western part of Austria near the Alps. Of the 2,000 who had started on the death march from Auschwitz, barely 400 had survived.

The SS unloaded us at the railroad station, from which they marched us up a long steep hill to the concentration camp. I have since learned that we arrived at Mauthausen on February 2, 1945.

As soon as we walked through the gate, a sergeant in the SS approached my brother and me. "Come with me," he crowed, "I need two strong men. I'll give you good jobs with plenty of food."

I was young and probably looked healthier than most of the wretches. "Can our father go with us?" I asked.

"No," he answered sharply, surprised that I would even dare to ask.

"Well, if we can't go with our father," I said, "we don't want the job."

The SS man was enraged by my insolence. He screamed, "Stupid, dirty Jew!" and smashed me on the head with his club. He split my scalp and blood gushed out. I still have the scar today.

As I held my bleeding wound, the SS sergeant promptly picked out two other prisoners, two boys with the first name of Meyer. The first Meyer was "the *Gayleh* Meyer," the same blond entertainer who sang songs for us in the Pionki camp. The second Meyer was a eunuch, castrated as part of some cruel Nazi medical experiment. He was very large and surprisingly fat compared to everyone else. Apparently, castration changes one's body chemistry so that food is metabolized differently. We later discovered that the "good jobs" intended for my brother and me were loading dead bodies to be burned in the crematorium—and the two boys named Meyer would both be murdered because they were eye-witnesses to war crimes.

After the SS sergeant walked away with the two Meyer boys, the guards drove the survivors of the death march into the showers. We were still wet when they pushed us outside into the open courtyard. There we stood naked in the dead of winter, shivering violently for eight long hours, while the Germans sprayed us every now and then with more freezing water. It was one more method that the SS used to kill off the weak. Finally, after an eternity of frigid waiting, they ordered us to run naked through the camp into a barrack. As we entered the barrack, each man received a pair of pants, a shirt, and shoes.

Some time later, we learned the reason that the Germans made us stand naked in the cold for so many hours. They could not move us into our assigned barrack until after they had completed a massacre. This barrack had once been filled with 600 high-ranking Russian officers, such as generals, colonels, majors and captains. Sensing that the Germans were at the brink of defeat, the Russians had attempted to revolt the day before. The Germans easily killed the leaders who tried to break out and then used machine-guns to massacre all the rest of the 600 Russian officers.

The Germans moved our group into the empty barrack for several days of quarantine. These few blessed days of rest were short-lived for my brother and me. On the third day, as punishment for refusing to take the crematorium job, we were singled out to bury the dead Russian officers. The SS took us to a long deep trench that would serve as a mass grave. The bodies of the Russian officers were already piled up near the grave. Our gruesome job was to strip the bodies, drag the 600 corpses into the trench, one at a time, and lay them in a row, head to toe, toe to head, covering each layer with lime. By now the corpses were already three or four days old and frozen stiff. The freezing cold prevented the bodies from stinking. But, we could easily see the carnage of the machine guns on the bodies, which were riddled everywhere with blood-caked bullet wounds—in the face, chest, limbs and head. A sane person cannot imagine what is was like to strip the corpses, drag the mutilated frozen bodies into the ditch, line them up, cover them with lime, and then lay another row of corpses on top of them. All you can do is try to shut your eyes and shut your mind. You go numb. From morning to night, my brother and I lay the bodies in the giant grave, layer after layer of dead Russian officers. Six hundred corpses. While my brother Joe and I worked, three other prisoners had an even worse job: they had to look in the mouths of the dead to extract gold teeth. It took us three days to complete the mass burial.

KL MAUTHAUSEN Kommandantur

Mauthausen, den 3. Februar 1945

Liste der Zugänge vom 2. Februar 1945

Auschwitz — Jaworzno

| 151. | Feldmann | Gitman | 1.5.21 | Suchedniow | Tischler-geh. | 125306 | Pole Jud |
| 152. | Feldman | Mendel | 5.7.97 | Suchedniow | Bäcker | 125307 | " |
| 153. | Ferrari | Giacomo | 19.11.08 | Busto Arsizio | Maurer | 125308 | It.Jeh. |
| 154. | Fessel | Maximilian | 14.1.08 | Wien | Werkzeugschloss. | 125309 | D..Jude |
| 155. | Feuerstein | Aron | 26.8.19 | Radowitz | Arbeiter | 125310 | Pole Jud |
| 156. | Finkielsztajn | Jakub | 19.4.04 | Radom | Tischler | 125311 | " |
| 157. | Finkielsztajn | Josef | 28.2.24 | Pulawy | Mont.Schloss. | 125312 | " |
| 158. | Finkiesztajn | Machel | 17.5.10 | Kielce | Elektriker | 125313 | " |
| 159. | Finkelstein | Markus | 8.4.11 | Krakau | Anstreicher | 125314 | " |
| 160. | Finkielsztajn | Salomon | 16.9.25 | Pulawy | Montageschlosser | 125315 | " |
| | | | | | | 125315 | " |
| 161. | Fiszbein | Aron | 24.5.25 | Warschau | Schlosser | 125316 | " |
| 162. | Fiszman | Szymon | 10.10.03 | Radom | Arbeiter | 125317 | " |
| 163. | Flam | Jordka | 11.12.26 | Kol biel | Elektriker | 125318 | " |
| 164. | Flagenbaum | Chaim | 30.12.25 | Radom | Schuster - Eisendreher | 125319 | " |
| 165. | Flamenbaum | Mendel | 10.4.10 | Jedlinsk | Socielan Schlosser | 125320 | " |
| 166. | Flamenbaum | Lukus | 25.6.20 | Radom | Arbeiter | 125321 | " |
| 167. | Fligelman | Mendel | 30.4.16 | Jedlisk | Schneider | 125322 | " |

This document is a Nazi concentration camp report of prisoner arrivals at Mauthausen. This is one segment from a 15-page list of 725 prisoners arriving at Mauthausen on February 2, 1945. Each page has 50 prisoners. Jacob, Joseph and Sol Finkelstein are entries #156, 157 and 160 on page 4. The spellings use standard Polish orthography, but without Polish diacritical marks (e.g., Jozef instead of Józef). In English translation, the entries read as follows:

156. Finkelsztajn Jakub, [DOB] 19 April 1904, [from] Radom, [occupation] carpenter (furniture maker), [inmate number] 125311, [nationality] Polish Jew.

157. Finkelsztajn Jozef, [DOB] 28 February 1924, [from] Puławy, [occupation] assembly fitter, [inmate number] 125312, [nationality] Polish Jew.

160. Finkelsztajn Salomon, [DOB] 16 September 1925, [from] Puławy, [occupation] assembly fitter, [inmate number] 125315, [nationality] Polish Jew.

# CHAPTER SIX

## Depths of the Earth

My father, brother and I remained at the Mauthausen main camp for about four weeks. Then, on March 7, 1945, the Germans selected two hundred prisoners and took us by train to a Mauthausen subcamp near Vienna, about 100 miles to the east. The Hinterbrühl concentration camp, a division of the Floridsdorf subcamp, was an ugly secret that few people have heard of. After the war, I learned it was originally a gypsum mine cut from a massive natural cave. They called it the "Sea Cave" because the mine had filled with water and formed the largest underground lake in Europe. The Nazis confiscated the cave, drained the water, and gave it to the Heinkel company to build a secret underground aircraft and rocket factory for the *Luftwaffe*. The cave provided perfect protection against Allied bombers and allowed the Germans to keep working on two secret weapons, which they hoped could still win the war for Germany. One was the infamous V2 rocket, the first long-range, high explosive war missile, and the other was the Heinkel HE 162 Salamander, one of the first jetfighters in the world.

Of course, we knew nothing of this when we arrived at Hinterbrühl. The barracks were built near the entrance to the old mine that housed the secret underground factory. Our group was added to the 1,800 prisoners who were already slaving and dying in the depths of the earth. All this was happening right in the middle of a quiet residential community in the district of Mödling, a suburb about eight miles outside of Vienna. Each day we would march into the mine and then descend some nine stories below the surface. The labor was continuous, 24 hours a day, with two shifts working 12 straight hours each day. Down in the mine, we didn't know day from night because it was so brightly illuminated with electric lights.

Veränderungsmeldung für den 7. M......

Von K.L. Mauthausen wurden nach dem Aussenkdo. FLORIDSDORF - für Hinterbrühl
folgende 200 Häftlinge lt. Aufstellung überstellt:

...ser: (8)

| | | | | | | |
|---|---|---|---|---|---|---|
| 1. | Holmann | Urban | 28.8.02 | Schwabeisen | 116824 | DR-Sch. |
| 2. | ...lien | Salomon | 15.6.03 | Saloniki | 130215 | Gr-Jude |
| 3. | Nimet | Pierre | 17.10.11 | Gentilly | 130389 | Fr-Sch. |
| 4. | Cyzan | Wilhelm | 8.5.24 | Krakau | 130517 | Poln.Jude |
| 5. | Danzig | Herman | 11.10.92 | Dunajska Strad. | 130534 | Slow.Sch. |
| 6. | Deutscher | Gustav | 26.9.22 | Krakau | 130556 | Poln.Jude |
| 7. | Eustache | Alfred | 29.4.11 | Granville | 130659 | Fr-Sch. |
| 8. | Grünthal | Heinz Isr. | 9.1.23 | Grossen | 130892 | DR-Jude |

Mechaniker: (2)

| | | | | | | |
|---|---|---|---|---|---|---|
| 9. | Hans | Franz | 8.12.14 | Wien | 116797 | DR-Sch. |
| 10. | Pierre | Aime | 18.2.16 | Tours | 128903 | Fr-Sch. |

Schlosser&Mechaniker: (5)

| | | | | | | |
|---|---|---|---|---|---|---|
| 11. | Gutman | Jerzy Israel | 20.5.23 | Warschau | 118814 | Poln.Jude |
| 12. | Albirt | Lejb | 1.6.15 | Kielce | 125165 | " |
| 13. | Nismer | Chaim | 12.7.19 | Mogielnica | 125210 | " |
| 14. | Golebiowski | Eljasz | 20.6.23 | Kielce | 125381 | " |
| 15. | Hubermann | Salama | 15.9.11 | Korzenica | 125437 | " |

Montage-Schlosser: (4)

| | | | | | | |
|---|---|---|---|---|---|---|
| 16. | Bogman | Momiek | 17.7.15 | Bielystok | 125236 | Poln.Jude |
| 17. | Bronstein | Moszek | 12.10.11 | Kozienice | 125253 | " |
| 18. | Finkielsztejn | Josef | 28.2.24 | Pulawy | 125312 | " |
| 19. | Finkielsztejn | Salama | 16.9.25 | Pulawy | 125315 | " |

Autoschlosser: (5)

| | | | | | | |
|---|---|---|---|---|---|---|
| 20. | Schoenheed | Philipp | 13.9.17 | Amsterdam | 125688 | Nl-Sch. |
| 21. | Brzezinski | Karol | 4.11.22 | Warschau | 130431 | Pole-Sch |
| 22. | Bulin | Wladimir | 20.6.26 | Jaroslawl | 130438 | Slv.Russe |
| 23. | Marylow | Akindia | 25.8.88 | Schuski | 130445 | " |
| 24. | Dechaitschow | Aleksander | 30.6.12 | Amrosenka | 130541 | " |

Maschinenschlosser: (34)

| | | | | | | |
|---|---|---|---|---|---|---|
| 25. | Pfleger | Johann | 21.2.06 | Wien | 119154 | DR-Sch. |
| 26. | Glusman | Abram | 15.11.13 | Lublin | 125363 | Poln.Jude |
| 27. | Graubart | Benjamin | 13.9.12 | Konskie | 125388 | " |
| 28. | Bendelss | Lejb | 3.3.15 | Lodz | 125420 | " |
| 29. | Bochman | Boruch | 4.2.26 | Litzmannstadt | 125431 | " |
| 30. | Horowics | Chaim | 6.10.95 | Lodz | 125434 | " |
| 31. | Hutter | Josef | 21.2.23 | Ealing | 125441 | Jugo-Sch |
| 32. | Katz | Elias | 25.2.15 | Nowy Targ | 125471 | Poln.Jude |
| 33. | Kurcz | Gersen | 10.3.20 | Radom | 125505 | " |
| 34. | Levy | Roland | 3.3.26 | Strassburg | 125527 | Fr-Sch. |
| 35. | Lewkowics | Jakob | 5.7.18 | Kielce | 125529 | Poln.Judd |
| 36. | Lipskye | Icek | 1.6.23 | Piotrkow | 125536 | " |
| 37. | Miedownik | David | 3.11.26 | Dabrowa | 125559 | " |
| 38. | Naftaniel | Harry | 8.8.15 | Graudenz | 125577 | DR-Sch. |
| 39. | Orenstein | Isaak | 17.2.16 | Optatow | 125584 | Poln.Jude |
| 40. | Pawlocki | Benisien | 20.6.14 | Warschau | 125590 | " |

These documents are two pages from a Nazi SS concentration camp list of prisoners transferred from the Mauthausen main camp to the Hinterbrühl subcamp on March 7, 1945. The names are organized by occupations. Joseph and Sol are listed as two of four *Montage-Schlosser* (assembly fitters) numbered 18 and 19. Jacob is listed on a separate page as a *Tischler* (carpenter), numbered 70. The documentation reads as follows:

Mauthausen Concentration Camp, Protective Custody Camp

Notice of Changes for March 7, 1945

The following 200 prisoners were transferred by arrangement from the Mauthausen Concentration Camp to the Extramural Work Detail at Floridsdorf for Hinterbrühl.

18. Finkielsztajn Josef, [DOB] 28 Feb 1924, [from] Pulawy, [inmate number] 125312, Polish Jew.
19. Finkielsztajn Salomon, [DOB] 16 Sep 1925, [from] Pulawy, [inmate number] 125315, Polish Jew.
70. Finkielsztajn Jakob, [DOB] 19 Apr 1904, [from] Radom, [inmate number] 125311, Polish Jew.

| | | | | | | |
|---|---|---|---|---|---|---|
| 53. | Schneider | Edward | 4.6.25 | Prag | 132888 | " |
| 54. | Stefanka | Paul | 7.5.24 | Turnowka | 132901 | " |
| 55. | Maliczewski | Josef | 1.6.21 | Palenica | 132974 | Pole Sch. |
| 56. | Babenko | Stepan | 2s.12.14 | Bredychino | 133016 | Ziv. Russe |
| 57. | Kaschin | Michail | 19.5.19 | Ufa | 133035 | " |
| 58. | Balery | Francois | 10.1.99 | Viroy | 133597 | Franz.Sch. |
| 50. | Frankel | Saymon | 18.8.15 | Kozienice | 125532 | Pole Jude |
| **Bohrer (1)** | | | | | | |
| 59. | Charmes | Jaques | 25.1.24 | Paris | 127664 | Franz.Sch |
| **Dreher (1)** | | | | | | |
| 60. | Zwifelhofer | Leopold | 8.11.13 | Wien | 117495 | DR.Sch. |
| **Former (1)** | | | | | | |
| 61. | Colle | Emile | 24.5.08 | Amiens | 127707 | Franz.Sch. |
| **Installateure (4)** | | | | | | |
| 62. | Dzmorak | Benedik | 29.1.14 | Rozindol | 130582 | Sl.Sch. |
| 63. | Englander | Rudi | 15.2.20 | Berlin | 130652 | DR.Jude |
| 64. | R C | Michal | 29.9.20 | Horva Jarka | 132775 | Slow.Sch. |
| 65. | Stole | Josef | 15.9.06 | Guberland | 132904 | Slow. Sch. |
| **Metallarbeiter (2)** | | | | | | |
| 66. | Duboi.. | Charles | 10.5.18 | Paris | 127800 | Franz. Sch. |
| 67. | Brycha | Vaclav | 24.9.16 | Telin | 130429 | Tsch.Boh. |
| **Tischler (29)** | | | | | | |
| 68. | Chimowics | Henryk | 14.3.26 | Litzmanstadt | 125570 | Pole Jude |
| 69. | Palimann | Gitman | 1.5.21 | Suchedmow | 125306 | " |
| 70. | Finkielsztajn | Jakob | 19.4.04 | Radom | 125311 | " |
| 71. | Libfeld | Josef | 20.2.10 | Kieloe | 125530 | " |
| 72. | Maiserstein | David | 16.3.18 | Opoczno | 125552 | " |
| 73. | Nathans | Erich | 8.5.13 | Leipzig | 125611 | DR.Jude |
| 74. | Stambach | Chaim | 6.5.15 | Ryoki | 125691 | Pole Jude |
| 75. | Ciecierski | Zenobiuss | 20.11.20 | Piotrkow. | 130070 | Pole Sch. |
| 76. | Ajzenberg | Moses | 27.12.04 | Rypin | 130581 | Pole Jude |
| 77. | Abanis | Christos | 3.8.06 | Alexandria | 130622 | Gr.Sch. |
| 78. | Bemmnis | Mikel.s | 8.10.09 | Semiten | 130298 | Let.Sch. |
| 79. | Bawol | Josef | 29.9.06 | Wyrozyze | 130301 | Pole Sch. |
| 80. | Berko | Deasü | 21.5.25 | Osepe | 130333 | Ung.Jude |

My job in the mine factory was to attach the guidance system near the nose of the V2 missiles. The V2s were huge, almost fifty feet long and five and half feet wide, suspended somehow so they could be moved around. To do my job, I had to lie on my back, high up on scaffolding, and use a screwdriver to mount the apparatus to the missile. I worked alone. One day, I actually fell asleep while doing my job. A German guard pulled me out and gave me a couple of kicks. He didn't hurt me, just scared me, and warned me not to fall asleep again.

We worked in the secret underground factory for about a month. My strongest memory is the pleasure we had when we came up out of the mine at the end of the work shift. By that time, American air power was absolutely dominant. We could see wave after wave after wave of American planes flying over and heard the rumbling of the bombs—and the once mighty Germans could do nothing to stop it. We all took heart that the Germans were closer to final defeat.

The advance of the Russian Army from the east forced the Germans to abandon the secret factory at Hinterbrühl. Without warning, the SS lined up every prisoner who could walk and started to march us out of the camp. We later learned that there were 51 prisoners in the infirmary who were too weak to walk. The Nazis murdered them by injecting gasoline into their hearts. On April 1, 1945, 1,884 prisoners, including my father, my brother and me, started a hundred mile death march back to the main Mauthausen concentration camp.

This second death march to Mauthausen was terrible. The weather in Austria is still extremely cold in the first week of April and we had no overcoats against the rain. We marched for seven agonizing days. We had no food except for scraps of grass we might occasionally find along the road; no water except where we found unmelted snow; no protection from the cold. Over two hundred men collapsed and were shot to death on the road. When the survivors finally reached Linz on April 8, 1945, the Germans made us wait until darkness before they marched us through the city. They did not want to disturb the Austrian civilians by exposing them to the sight of 1,600 nearly dead, emaciated Jews. [4]

After re-entering the main Mauthausen concentration camp, the Germans locked our wretched group in Block 24 for five days of quarantine. Once each day, the SS unlocked the gate and some prisoners carried in a large kettle of weak soup. That was our reward for trudging one hundred miles through the cold and rain.

On the second day, while everyone was attending to the soup, I had the sudden impulse to escape. I slipped unnoticed through the unlocked gate and

---

[4]    The commanding officers of Hinterbrühl were later convicted of war crimes for the brutality of this death march.

walked into the main concentration camp. Having no plan, I simply wandered around the camp until I picked one barrack at random and entered.

It turned out that this barrack was occupied by former Republican fighters from the Spanish Civil War. Nearly all of them were Communists, mostly Spanish, quite a few Italians, and a handful of French. There were no Jews among them. After losing to General Francisco Franco in the Spanish Civil War in 1939, these Spanish men had fled to France where they were later arrested by the Germans and sent to prison at Mauthausen in 1940. Most of the Italians had been arrested for opposing Mussolini. The Spanish and Italians had survived imprisonment at Mauthausen for so many years that they had earned the most important, "prominent" jobs in the camp. So they were called "Prominents." Since Spanish and Italian are based on Latin, and I had learned Latin in school, I tried to communicate with them in broken Latin. This was quite amusing to the Prominents, who laughed and corrected my words. They liked me.

"All right," they said, "You can come and work for us. You'll clean our latrines."

"But I'm in the quarantine," I replied.

"What are you doing here?"

"I escaped."

"How did you do that?" they asked.

"I slipped through the gate when they weren't looking."

"Well, you shouldn't do that again. It's too dangerous." Instead they explained that I could pose as a Prominent by switching my yellow Jewish badge for a red badge. Political prisoners, like these Communists from the Spanish Civil War, wore red badges. Criminals wore green. Jews wore yellow. I don't remember where I eventually found two red badges, but I stole them along with two hats. Wearing a hat with a visor was another sign of importance in Mauthausen.

Pleased with my success, I snuck back into the quarantine block and gave one hat and one red badge to my brother Joe. Instantly, we changed from Jews into Prominents. We simply walked out of the quarantine block, and moved into the barrack with the Spanish and Italians. They took me in as a mascot, a pet boy, and we cleaned the latrines. Compared to the Jewish prisoners at Mauthausen, the Prominents had plenty of bread and food. Our possibilities of survival increased tremendously by not being identified as Jews.

Joe and I would take our extra bread back to the Jewish barracks and give it to my father and our friends. We had so much bread that my father was actually trading bread for cigarettes. We felt like we were rich.

One day, I traded for soup, and retrieved a kettle that had been placed for me between the double electric wire fences that surrounded Mauthausen. During the day the wires were not electrified. The electricity was turned on at 4 p.m. every day, on a schedule, and kept on overnight for about 16 hours until sunrise, then turned off again during the daylight hours. I entered the small space between the two wire fences at around 2 p.m., and grabbed the kettle. I turned to walk back out, and suddenly the electrical wiring was activated earlier than the normal schedule. I could hear the deadly crackle of electricity in the wires on both sides of me. I was left standing in the narrow space between the two live electrical fences, holding the kettle of soup. I was unable to move an inch and stood perfectly still. It looked like I would have to stand there until the wires were deactivated the next morning. I feared I would be shot if a guard spotted me standing between the two fences. Then, about five minutes later, the wires went silent, the crackling and humming sounds stopped, and the electricity was turned off. It was some sort of test. I moved out quickly with the soup.

Having adequate food was a godsend, but there was one day that it was not. My father, brother and I were walking outside, and one of the SS guards suddenly attacked us. He cursed and beat us with a club, screaming, "*Sein Sohn eines gut gefütterten Zimmermannes?!*" "You're a well-fed carpenter's son." He beat us simply because we were not as skinny and emaciated as the other prisoners.

Vicious beatings from the guards were common at Mauthausen. Although my brother and I had an easier life than the other prisoners, it was a horrible, brutal concentration camp with starvation, sickness and death. The SS guards devised all sorts of cruel games to humiliate and kill Jews and others. A special form of Nazi cruelty became known after the war ended. The Mauthausen quarry was the site of one of their favorite killing games. They would make the prisoners carry very heavy stones on their backs, sometimes 60 to 100 pounds, up a long set of stone stairs. Climbing in single file, the prisoners had to climb 186 "Stairs of Death" to reach the top of the quarry. If a man was too weak to make it, he would collapse under the weight and tumble down the stairs, which would crush the other prisoners climbing below him. They would all fall to their deaths. If a prisoner actually reached the top of the stairs, he would throw the stone down and then have to go back down to carry up another stone. Many men could not endure this agony and would just leap to their deaths into the quarry. The SS guards thought this was very funny. "Parachutists without parachutes," they laughed.

Great numbers of prisoners just died slowly from starvation, illness and exhaustion—like Yurik Neuman. He was my brother's high school friend, who was with us in Pionki, tattooed with us when we arrived at Auschwitz, and made the same death march with us to Mauthausen. Like us, Yurik had survived every Nazi ordeal since the Radom ghetto. But the relentless strain of starvation had slowly destroyed his body and spirit. One night I went to sleep with Yurik beside me. When I awoke the next morning, Yurik was dead. Sadly, of the three Neuman brothers, only one survived the Holocaust.

Death was so frequent at Mauthausen that the camp had its own crematorium. It was not designed for mass burnings like Auschwitz, but there were four small ovens that could burn two bodies at a time. Smoke was continuously rising from the crematorium chimney at Mauthausen, always carrying the smell of death.

Toward the end of the war, the Nazis were slaughtering hundreds of thousands of Hungarian Jews. Most went to the ovens at Auschwitz, but after closing Auschwitz, the Nazis sent thousands of Hungarian Jews to Mauthausen. In April, 1945, there were not enough barracks to hold the Hungarian Jews, so the SS set up a tent camp, a *Zeltlager*, just outside the main camp. The non-Jewish main camp was on top of a steep hill, and the Jewish tent camp was down at the bottom of the hill. Since the Hungarians had come directly from their homes, they still carried their suitcases, and wore civilian clothes, makeup and jewelry. Many of the Hungarian newcomers were still with their wives and children.

After a while, the Nazis moved my father and the other Jews from the quarantine block into the tent camp with the Hungarian Jews. All the Jews at Mauthausen were ordered into the lower tent camp, and all the non-Jews stayed in the upper main camp. There were thousands of Jews crowded into the tent camp and they suffered terribly from starvation, exposure and disease. Luckily, wearing our caps and red badges, my brother Joe and I were seen as non-Jewish Prominents, so we were not forced into the tent camp with the other Jews. We hated to be separated from our father but, as Prominents, we could move freely around the camp and could supply him with better food rations. In addition, one of the Prominents also said he would keep an eye on Father and let us know if anything happened.

After that, we visited Father in the tent camp every day. During this period, my brother and I also made friends with a Czech political prisoner, who was the accountant for the camp. He lived in the same block with the Spaniards and knew we were Jewish, but he did a lot to help me. One day, a Hungarian gave me two watches for food. I walked up the hill and gave them to the block leader, who gave me four loaves of bread and a pound of butter. I then went back down to the tent camp and gave the man three loaves of bread, and half of the butter. Then I kept one loaf and the remaining butter to share with my father and friends. So we developed a sort of charitable business with the Czech and the other Prominents. Joe and I would bring bread, butter, sugar and soup down to the starving Hungarians in the tent camp, which we would "pay" for by trading their watches and jewelry for food. Then we would climb back up the hill to give the valuables to the Prominents, who would give us more bread and then the Prominents would sell the valuables to the German guards.

For about two weeks, we were able to help our father and the other Jews in this way. But then one of the SS Commanders caught my brother and me carrying a full kettle of soup down to the Hungarian camp. He knocked the soup onto the ground and beat the hell out of me, screaming *"Juden Freunde!"* "Jew friend!" He would have surely killed me if he knew I was Jewish, but I was wearing the hat and red badge of a Prominent. He beat me viciously for bringing food to the Jews. Finally, I left the kettle on the ground and simply ran away. Luckily, the German Commander let me go. He could have had me executed.

Although I survived this beating, it marked the beginning of a series of dreadful events. On April 16, and again on April 26, the SS took large groups of Jews from the Mauthausen tent camp and marched them out to who knows where. Then, on April 28, 1945, we heard a rumor that the Germans were planning to liquidate the remaining people from the tent camp. My father said to me and my brother, "Go back up to the main camp and get yourselves some food. Save yourselves if you can. I don't want to lose my whole family."

"No, Father," I said, "We're not going to leave you. We'll just go up, get whatever food we can, and come right back."

"Fine," my father agreed.

Joe and I went back up the hill to the main camp, but shortly thereafter, before we could go back to Father, the SS suddenly ordered a *Blocksperrung*, a lockdown. They cordoned off the tent camp, locked everyone in their barracks and no one was allowed to go in or out. We were powerless to help Father as the Germans quickly took everyone out of the tent camp and started a forced march. Our father was gone, taken with all of the other Jews in the lower camp. We later learned that the Nazis planned to march them into some tunnels near Gusen, Austria, then blow it up to kill them all and conceal the massacre, but the Nazis never carried out this plan. All I knew at the time was that I had lost my father, and my brother Joe was now falling ill with deadly typhus. Joe became so sick that he could no longer walk. He lay in his bunk helpless. He was too weak to lift one arm to take a spoonful of water, so I had to feed him water with a spoon. It looked like he was going to die. I didn't know what to do except stay close and try to help.

A week later, I felt the early symptoms of typhus creeping into my own body. On May 5th, at nine o'clock in the morning, the Czech accountant came looking for me. "Zolomon," that's what he called me, "You have to hide. The Germans are abandoning the camp, but first they're going to kill you. They already shot the two boys named Meyer who worked in the crematorium. Now they're looking for you. You two are witnesses. You buried the Russians in the mass grave."

I had to act quickly. My brother Joe was so weak, he couldn't even lift his head. And I was rapidly getting ill myself. I had no choice but to pick him up and carry him. I managed to carry him all the way to the infirmary, where I begged for help from the Polish doctor who was in charge.

"Doctor, please save us. My brother is sick and I'm sick and the SS are looking for us because we're witnesses. Please send us down to the hospital."

"I can't," he replied. "The camp is locked down. No one can get to the hospital."

"Please help us," I begged again.

"I can't do anything. The only thing I can tell you is we have a little mortuary here where we keep the bodies before we send them away. You could try to hide there."

I just stared at him and he turned away. The mortuary was the only choice. With my last remaining strength, I somehow half-carried, half-dragged my brother to the mortuary. If the SS found us, they would kill us instantly—just like they had murdered the two Meyers, who had taken the crematorium jobs that had been intended for us.

I struggled until we reached the morgue, a tiled room with dozens of corpses heaped on the floor. I closed the door, pulled the corpses apart, placed my brother on the floor between them, and covered him with the dead.

I pushed another gap between the dead bodies, lay down, and pulled two corpses over myself. The dead were not heavy, their emaciated remains were only skin and bones. But their bones pressed against my own bones.

I lay as quietly as I could, covered by the dead, listening for the boots of the SS. The only sound was my own breathing, sharp and rapid from my exertion and terror. It was like the prophecy of Ezekiel in the valley of dry bones, Ezekiel 37:1-6.

> *The Lord set me down in the midst of the valley. It was full*
> *of bones . . .*

How did I come to be in such a place? What had become of the world? Was there any hope in this desolation of bones?

And God told Ezekiel to speak to the bones thus:

> *Dry bones, hear the word of the Lord . . . I will cause breath*
> *to enter you, and you shall live again. I will lay sinews upon you,*
> *and cover you with flesh, and form skin over you. I will put breath*
> *into you, and you shall live again . . .*

My brother and I stay hidden for an eternity, two hours that seemed like two thousand, beneath the cold corpses. But the Germans did not find us. Eventually, I heard a siren blow, and the Polish doctor came back to tell us that the Germans were gone, and it was safe. I dared to crawl out from my hiding place and I freed my brother as well. It was five-and-a-half years since the Germans had entered Radom and our suffering first began. I was only 14 years old when it started. I was now 19, and weighed 88 pounds. I was nothing more than a living skeleton.

Once again, God had personally saved my life within minutes of execution—like the stolen gasoline at the SS garage and the stolen linens at Sosnowiec. This time, two hours before liberation, God sent the Czech to warn me to hide from the Nazi executioners.

# CHAPTER SEVEN

## From the Valley of Bones

My brother Joe and I climbed out from the grave to find ourselves liberated at last—by General Patton's 11th Armored Division of the American Army. It was a wild scene as the American tanks drove into Mauthausen. I was too weak to celebrate with the other prisoners, but I watched them screaming with joy as they mobbed the tank. The people were so thrilled that they started throwing the tank commander into the air. They nearly killed him with their hurrahs of happiness. Then a second American tank drove in, following by a third and a fourth. It was 11:00 in the morning on a bright sunny day, May 5, 1945. We were free.

Thin as a rake, and starting to feel the wooziness of typhus myself, I was more stunned than exultant about being liberated. When your body is starved and weakened to the brink of death, it is hard to feel joy. My immediate concern was to save my brother by getting him medical help. Then I must find our father, who had been marched out of Mauthausen one week before. Hopefully, he was still alive.

Events were chaotic after liberation. Before the American Army could gain control, the former prisoners were taking revenge on the former guards and *kapos*. They were dragging them out, one at a time, and letting the mob beat them to death. The former prisoners took one of the most vicious and hated guards and boiled him alive.

Meanwhile, for the first time in the history of Mauthausen camp, the Swiss Red Cross was given permission to give care packages to the prisoners. As quickly as the Red Cross brought the packages in the gate, the prisoners attacked and ripped the boxes apart. I was in the crowd and managed to snatch some chocolate, raisins and a pound cake. I brought the sweets to my brother

Joe, but he was so ill that he could not eat a single bite of the delicious food. I knew I had to get medical help for Joe while I was still strong enough to do it. I was becoming sicker with typhus myself. By then, the Americans put up barbed wire fences and were trying to quarantine sections of the camp to prevent the spread of epidemic diseases. Typhus was raging through the camp and huge numbers of people were sick or becoming sick. I dragged my sick brother to the Polish doctor in the dispensary and begged for help.

"You have typhus," the Polish doctor said, "I can't keep you here. You have to go down to the hospital because you're carrying an infectious disease. They have a typhus unit there."

I refused. "Doctor we're not going down there. We're Jews. We'll die in that place." The chief doctor of the hospital was an anti-Semitic Yugoslav, who didn't care if a Jew lived or died. I did not trust that we could be given proper medical care.

The doctor was understanding. "I'll try to protect you," he said. "I'll write special medical orders for you."

The so-called hospital was down the hill from the main camp and we were too weak to walk there. Then my brother pulled out two gold coins that he had sewn into his hat for safekeeping. We had earned the coins during the period when we were trading jewelry for bread with the Hungarian Jews in the tent camp.

"Listen," my brother said to the doctor, "We will do as you say. But I don't know if we will live or die. Here are two gold coins. Our name is Finkelstein."

The doctor told my brother his name, which was a Polish name I can't remember, and spoke in a kind voice. "After things settle down, I'm going back to my town in Poland. If you survive, you can come to see me there, and I'll give you the coins back." Then the doctor called in another fellow and gave him a written order. "Take these two Jewish boys, the Finkelstein brothers, down to the hospital."

I followed the fellow, dragging my poor brother because he was still too weak to walk. When the fellow opened the gate, I had a sudden change of heart. I stopped and sat down.

"No," I said, thinking of the anti-Semitism that had always dominated Poland and Europe, "I'm not going down there because they'll kill us. Even though we've been liberated, we're still Jews. The other prisoners are all non-Jews. If they find out, we'll die, or be killed."

The fellow looked at me with an odd expression and started to cry. "No, they will not kill you," he said reassuringly. "I'm Jewish too. I have been pretending to be a Pole all this time." Not a person in the world knew that this fellow was Jewish until the moment he told us. "Don't worry, Finkelsteins, the Polish doctor there is a friend of mine because we were together in the Polish uprising in Warsaw in August, 1944. I'll make sure that you'll be taken good care of."

The Jewish fellow then helped us to make it to the camp hospital. There he found the chief doctor, and said, "Doctor, these two Jewish boys are friends of mine. You must take very good care of these boys."

That same afternoon, the Polish doctor came back with a short little Jewish doctor from Detroit, maybe five-feet tall, named Dr. Friedman. He was a U.S. Army physician and knew enough Yiddish that we could converse. "Look," he said, "They survived Hitler and they'll survive here. I'll make you responsible." He said the name of the American major in charge of the camp, and told the doctor we were the major's cousins. "Tell me what you need and I'll make sure you get it."

The Polish doctor did exactly that. He made it his business to visit us every two hours to make sure that we were being taken care of. In fact, we were the only patients who received hospital beds in the typhus quarantine unit. All the other patients lay on straw mattresses on the floor. Better yet, we were the only patients who received injections of penicillin every morning. And that was not all that he did. One day the Polish doctor brought a little bottle of red medicine and said, "Here, give a spoonful of this to your brother every two hours." It turned out to be red wine. I did as the doctor ordered and Joseph was able to recover from the typhus. That red wine really seemed to help, because he was out of bed in just a few days.

Thankfully, my typhus was not as severe as my brother's so I had been able to take care of him. But then I came down with pleurisy. Pleurisy fills your lungs with fluid, making it painful and difficult to breathe. It is a life-threatening illness. At one point, I weighed only 40 kilograms, which is about 88 pounds. I was nothing but skin and bones, as close to being dead as you can get. Fortunately, my brother was now strong enough to take care of me. Given the severity of my condition, Dr. Friedman transferred me to an American Army hospital in the nearby village of Gusen, and he checked on me every day to be sure I was okay.

Even with the best of care, it took me five months to recover from pleurisy. By now, the doctors knew that too much food could kill a starvation victim, so my food was restricted to nothing but saltine crackers and clear soup broth. I was hungry enough to eat a horse, but all I got was saltines. My brother Joe stayed close by to take care of me in the hospital. I believe I was among the very few survivors to actually receive an antibiotic. At that time the Americans had penicillin, but the Europeans didn't. Without the special care that we received from the Polish doctor, we probably would have died along with the hundreds of other prisoners who died after liberation from malnutrition and typhus. Once again, God had provided a human angel to save my life—this time in the form of the secret Jewish prisoner at Mauthausen, who was friends with the good Polish doctor.

Liberation was not a happy experience for my brother and me. We deeply regretted our choice to separate from our father in the last hours of Mauthausen concentration camp and were haunted by thoughts of what may have happened to him. Our sense of dread increased as more weeks passed and we heard nothing about him. We sought whatever bits of information we could find to piece together the story of his final days. Eventually we determined that Father had survived the death march with the Hungarian Jews that had evacuated Mauthausen on April 28, 1945. My understanding, for years, was that he and the Hungarian Jews had been marched into another concentration camp, which was called Gusen. There, I believed, my father lived to see liberation on May 4, 1945, but perished a few days later from starvation.

For the next sixty-three years, I was haunted by the uncertain circumstances of my father's death. I believed that I should have never left him alone in the Mauthausen tent camp, and that I could have helped him to survive if we had stayed together. So, I felt personally responsible. I did not even know his exact date of death in order to say *Kaddish* for him (the Jewish prayer of mourning). It was a terrible question mark that weighed on my conscience and gave me nightmares. I could never forgive myself for not being with my father at the end.

Thankfully, something extraordinary happened during the course of writing this book, which has totally changed my life. In July, 2008, thanks to his diligent efforts, my son, Joseph, was able to obtain documentation from researchers at the U.S. Holocaust Memorial Museum that finally answered the questions of my father's death. This is what I learned:

My father, Jacob Noah Finkelstein, was marched out of Mauthausen tent camp with the other Jewish prisoners, mostly Hungarians, on April 28, 1945. This was the last of three evacuations from Mauthausen, which occurred on April 16, 26, and 28. My father survived the march of about 25 miles to Gunskirchen concentration camp (not Gusen as I had thought). The Gunskirchen camp was in a forest about three miles west of the small city of Wels, Austria. About 6,000 Jews died during the three death marches from Mauthausen tent camp, but the survivors of the last march, my father's group, probably arrived at Gunskirchen on May 2nd or 3rd. By then, the camp was in horrendous disorder, jammed with as many as 17,000 prisoners. Barracks that were built for only 300 were now crammed with 2,500 prisoners each, and prisoners were denied food for five days. The water supply was nil, diarrhea was rampant and the capacity of the latrines was completely overwhelmed.

On May 4th, the SS fled the camp as the 71st Infantry Division of the American Army approached. When the American Army liberated the camp on May 5, 1945, they were horrified by the conditions at Gunskirchen. The prisoners looked like scarecrows. Hundreds of bodies were strewn over the grounds. The stench of feces, urine, and dead corpses was unbearable.

The Americans began transporting many survivors, including my father, to a hospital in the nearby city of Wels. My dear father died in a hospital bed in Wels, on May 8, 1945, just four days after liberation. The hospital records, written in German, said his cause of death was "inflammation of the kidney basin, large intestine and heart muscle." Doctors tell me this was most likely the result of typhus.

My father was buried in a section of the municipal cemetery of Wels, along with a total of 1035 Jewish Holocaust survivors of Gunskirchen who died in Wels after liberation.

For the next 56 years, these graves at Wels cemetery were just a field of unmarked, open grass, except for a handful of individual markers that had been added by families. In 2001, the City of Wels dedicated a memorial to the Holocaust victims from Gunskirchen buried in Wels cemetery. The memorial consists of a narrow glass plate pillar and two vertical glass walls, on which are inscribed the known names of the victims, including my father.

After 63 years, I finally know what happened to Father. I now know the exact day to say the *Kaddish* prayer for Father's *Yahrzeit*, the anniversary of his death.

My son Joseph has placed a gravestone in Wels cemetery, marking my father's final resting place.

May Jacob Finkelstein's memory be for a blessing.

Summer and winter photographs of the 2001 Wels Cemetery Memorial. The two glass walls list the known names of the 1,035 victims who died in Wels, Austria, after the liberation of Gunskirchen. Listed in alphabetical order, the name of Jakob Finkelstein appears at mid-height on the 17th line of the left panel.

EMILIE DEUTSCH ○ GEORGI DEUTSCH ○ JAKOB DEUTSCH
ZSÖ ○ MICHAEL DEZSÖ ○ BELA DIRFTAG ○ IMRE DOZSA
NBERGER ○ LIPOT EINHORN ○ JOSEF (EESI) EISE ○ LEOPOI
○ DANIEL ENGEL ○ DAVID ENGEL ○ JOSEF ENGEL ○ SANDO
ENDRE FARKAS ○ IMRE FARKAS ○ ISAK FARKAS ○ ISTVA
I FEINTUK ○ BELA FEIZLER ○ ANTON FELDMANN ○ KAROL
IALY FEURERER ○ JAKOB FINKELSTEIN ○ ANDOR FISCHER ○
IEZSO FISCHER ○ SUSCMANN FISCHER ○ LASZLO FISCHL ○
○ KAROLY FÖLDES ○ LASZLO FÖLDES ○ DR. ISTVAN FORNA ○
EL FRENKEL ○ MARTON FRENKEL ○ ALADOR FRENKI ○ GEZA
RIEDMANN ○ LAZAR FRIEDMANN ○ MARKUS FRIEDMANN ○
RISCHMANN ○ GYULA FROMME ○ MARTON FUCHS ○ OTTO
Z ○ JANOS GAROSIKI ○ ANDOR GASPAR ○ SULTAN GELB ○
INA ○ JOSEF GIER ○ GEZA GLÜCK ○ JANOS GLÜCK ○ ISAK
ROTEIN ○ BELA GOLDSTEIN ○ ISTVAN GOLDSTEIN O

The top photo is a close-up of the left panel of the Wels memorial, which includes the name of Jakob Finkelstein (center).

The bottom photo shows the new gravestone which was placed on the site of Jacob Finkelstein's grave at Wels Cemetery in December, 2008.

יעקב נח בן בן-ציון
פינקלשטיין
JACOB NOAH FINKELSTEIN
19.4.1898 - 8.5.1945

In September, 1945, while I was still recuperating in the hospital in Gusen, we heard the wonderful rumor that my mother and sister Ann had survived the war together and were back in Poland. Although I had regained some strength, I was still too weak to travel, so my brother Joe traveled alone to Poland. Three weeks later, Joe returned to confirm that the story was true! Mother and Ann were alive! It had been over a year since the day I last saw them—separated at the train platform in Auschwitz. I learned that my mother and sister had been imprisoned together in four concentration camps—Bomlitz, Bergen-Belsen, Elsnig and Buchenwald. On one occasion, while they were being transported by train to yet another camp, the Allies, thinking the train was a German troop train, bombed the transport. Many Jewish prisoners died. Ann and my mother ran off the train into the woods, where they were later liberated by the Russians, on April 28, 1945.

After their liberation, my mother and sister returned to our hometown of Radom to see if anyone else had survived. They only stayed in Radom for two days because there were strong anti-Semitic feelings in Radom and there were reports of Poles murdering Jews who had returned home after the war. Instead, my mother and sister traveled from Radom to the city of Lodz, where it was a bit safer for Jews. They found only a few distant cousins who had survived the war, but they stayed in Lodz, hoping that one of us would also return home.

During his trip to Poland, my brother went to see the kind Polish doctor from Mauthausen, who had helped to save us. Just as he had promised, the doctor had saved the two gold coins that my brother had entrusted to him. After returning home to Poland, the doctor put the coins in an envelope, wrote "Finkelstein" on it, locked it in his safe, and waited for the day that we might return. The Polish doctor was a true *mensch*—an honorable, honest, compassionate person. This experience was amazing, so unlike the Polish anti-Semitism we usually encountered.

As soon as my brother brought the wonderful news to me in Austria, we made arrangements to travel back to Lodz. It was now October, 1945. When I was finally discharged from the Army hospital in Gusen, Rosh Hashanah had passed and I was 20 years old. I went to the local authorities to get an *ausweisser*, which are identification papers like a passport. Since we knew it was still dangerous to be Jew in Poland, I said my name was "Joachim Tanzer" from Germany. Tanzer was the name of a German who I had worked for in the ghetto. It was that easy. So then I went to another office and obtained another set of identification papers. This time I said I was a Pole by the name of "Justakowicz," which I stole from a newspaper article. I wasn't sure which identity would be better. Then my brother and I hopped on the train for Poland. At that time, the borders were still wide open and displaced persons could travel anywhere by train for free—as long as you could squeeze aboard. So off we went from Gusen,

Austria to Lodz, Poland. It's funny, but sometime during the trip, someone stole both of my fake identity papers.

Finally, we reached Lodz and I had a joyful reunion with my mother and sister. I remember that I had the most delicious meal of my whole life on my first day there. It was a simple piece of challah bread with farmer cheese and a sliced pear. After all those years in concentration camps and five months of saltine crackers in the Gusen hospital, I never imagined something could taste so fabulous! I still have the *tam*, the taste, of that first breakfast with my mother. I never believed the world could be so wonderful as a piece of challah with farmer cheese and a sliced pear.

We stayed in Lodz for about three weeks and discussed what we should do. "Well, we're not staying in Poland," my mother declared. "I can't stand the Poles. All they want to know is how any of us Jews could possibly survive the camps. They wanted us all to burn."

At one point, my mother said she wanted to run away and convert to Christianity.

"Mother, why?" I asked.

"I don't want you or your children ever to be confronted with the penalty of being Jewish. I don't want to be near Jews. I don't want to hear the word Jew. I want to get away from it as far as the moon."

Such was my mother's grief over losing her husband and two children, and seeing the senseless horrors of the war. She was doubting the value of continuing to live a Jewish life.

Thank goodness that we did not surrender to that despair. There is a Hebrew phrase (1 Samuel 15:29) that says, *"Netzach Yisrael lo ishaker."* The strength of Israel is eternal. The continuity of Jewish people will never fade. The Jewish chain will continue, as it has for five thousand years.

But not in Poland. For us, Poland was a cursed country. There was nothing Jewish left. Even though Jews had been erased from the land, the Poles still hated us. We decided we would emigrate to Israel—and the way to get to Israel was to go through one of the Displaced Persons (DP) camps in Germany. So we took a train from Lodz, Poland to Prague, Czechoslovakia, and from there, we planned to go to Germany.

In Prague, we stayed in a refugee hotel for about three weeks, while we gathered information and made plans for the next connection. We learned that a large number of Jews from our hometown of Radom were now gathered in a Displaced Persons camp in Stuttgart, Germany, so this seemed like the best place to go to find friends and family.

How did so many Jews from Radom end up in Stuttgart? It turned out that many Radomers had been imprisoned in a concentration camp called Vaihingen an der Enz, which is just outside of Stuttgart. After liberation, General

Eisenhower himself asked the citizens of Stuttgart to provide some shelter for the poor Jewish refugees from the concentration camp. But the local people were selfish and complained. This angered General Eisenhower, so he decided to do the same thing to the Germans that they had done to the Jews. The U.S. Army confiscated a small section of Stuttgart on a hill to create a Displaced Persons camp.

"You have 24 hours to get out," Eisenhower said to the Germans. "Take your personal belongings, but leave the furniture, the china, the silverware, and everything else so the Jews can have a home." That was the start of it. There were rows of apartment buildings along Bismarck Street, three and four stories high on both sides. Most of the Radomers from the Vaihingen-Enz camp moved into the vacated apartments. Then, as word spread that there were Radomers in Stuttgart, more and more survivors from Radom traveled there until eighty percent of the people in the DP camp were originally from Radom.

Unfortunately, during our three-week stay in Prague, my brother contracted scarlet fever. The Czech government immediately put Joe into quarantine to prevent the spread of epidemic illness. My mother and sister wanted to go ahead to Stuttgart. "I'm not going to leave Joe," I declared. "I survived the war with him and I'm not going to leave him alone here."

So my mother and sister left for Stuttgart and I stayed in Prague until Joe recovered. This was not easy because I only had a transit visa, and the Red Cross would not issue papers unless I had employment in Czechoslovakia. So I got a job with an architectural firm and used my fake German name of Joachim Tanzer. I learned Czech very quickly because it is similar to Polish and was able to communicate quite well. My employer gave me pay, food coupons and a visa to stay in Prague. I told my boss that I was staying only until my brother was released from the hospital. But the hospital would not let me visit Joe because of the quarantine. All I could do for him was to bring a couple of apples each day. That's all Joe wanted and that's all they would allow.

Eventually my brother recovered and was released from the hospital. By then, I was enjoying my job. This was my first paid job in my whole life and it felt good to earn money. My employer trusted me, liked my work and paid very well to keep me. In fact, he knew my mother, who agreed that it was okay for me to stay for a little while longer. But Joe was eager to rejoin the family. We had an ugly argument before he left.

Two weeks later, I began to feel lonely. Earning money was not worth separation from my family. So I started making arrangements to go to Germany. Before I set off, however, I encountered a beautiful Hungarian woman and her husband, who were also going there. They offered to bring me along—as long as I agreed to carry some contraband cigarettes. As luck would have it, we were stopped and arrested at the border by the Czech police. They accused the Hungarian couple of being some sort of counter-revolutionary spies or something called "Februarists."

"Look," I explained in Czech, "I'm not a smuggler or a spy. I'm just trying to get to my family in Germany. I was only here because my brother was quarantined in the hospital and I'll be damned if I'm going to be stuck in Czechoslovakia." I told them the honest truth that I was a Jewish survivor and showed them the Auschwitz number tattooed on my forearm.

"Why go to Germany?" the Czech police asked me. "The Germans persecuted you."

"The Poles are just as bad to the Jews as the Germans," I replied. "We are planning to go from Germany to Israel."

The lieutenant in charge had pity on me. "All right, let him go."

But then I had a clever idea. "Not only do I want you to let me through the border," I said, "but I want you to *escort* me across."

The Czechs were amused by my demand. Sure enough, the lieutenant from the border patrol escorted me across the border and bought me a ticket on the German railroad so I could go to Stuttgart and rejoin my family. I must say the Czechs were very nice people. They were kind to Jews during the war and they were unbelievably nice to displaced persons like me.

I finally arrived at Stuttgart in November of 1945 and moved into a house at 188 Bismarck Street with my mother, brother and sister. My health was fully restored. Just like Ezekiel's promise, God had lifted me up from the grave at Mauthausen, breathed life into me, and lay sinews and flesh upon my bones. After so much pain and loss, it was time to enjoy life. Sadly, my father, and my brothers Abraham and Aaron were gone but, compared to most Jewish families, we were lucky that four of us had somehow survived. So many of the Jews in the Stuttgart camp had lost most or all of their families. There were no young children or older people there. The DP camp was dominated by youth and young adults, so romances were springing up like flowers everywhere. Many others had lost their husbands and wives during the war. It was like everyone was in a hurry to catch up for the lost years and begin new lives. There were many Jewish weddings.

It was also a time of renewed passion about Zionism. Like many survivors, I was excited by the new opportunity to emigrate to Israel and make the Zionist dream into reality. After coming to the DP camp in Stuttgart, it was natural to join with other Jews who felt the same pride and hope. I remembered how much I enjoyed the Zionist groups from my youth in Radom and it gave me the idea of creating a communal place in Stuttgart where Jews could meet socially, learn Jewish traditions and build Jewish pride. There were other men in the DP camp, who were older and more important than me, but I had the idea and gave them the push to get it started.

That was how we created the *Beit Bialik* (House of Bialik), which was named after the famous Jewish poet Chaim Nachman Bialik. It had a Jewish school and a library where people could come to read books and newspapers, or just meet and talk. There were also many teenagers, so I had the idea of creating a Jewish youth group that would be open to everyone, not just partisan groups. So we named it the Zionist United Jewish Group, or *Nocham* for short. The *Nocham* offered classes and seminars as well as Jewish camps for the youth. Even the chief secretary for the famous psychoanalyst Alfred Adler was there to teach us about the psychological theories of Freud, Jung and Adler. Learning about the unconscious mind was fascinating. It was an exciting time. The idea of the *Nocham* worked so well that it became a model for every Jewish DP camp in Germany.

Reviving Judaism and rebuilding Jewish pride was a great accomplishment in the wake of the destruction of European Jewry. But there was also an ugly incident in Stuttgart that helped to build Jewish unity in Stuttgart. In the early days of the DP camp, many of the Jewish refugees traded in the black market because no one had any money and there were no jobs. Even my mother, who was a very smart businesswoman before the war, was making money in the black market. We were all buying and selling and trading. It was normal. But the authorities did not like it. So, on March 29, 1946, the German police conducted a big raid of the Jewish homes in Stuttgart. Even though the Stuttgart DP camp was called a "camp," it was inside the city proper and consisted of blocks of apartment buildings that had been requisitioned by Eisenhower and the U.S. Army for use by Jewish refugees. So when the German police raided the camp, they were charging into our personal homes—just like the Nazis used to do. The German police were banging on doors, dragging Jews from their homes, and even shot and killed a friend of ours in front of his family. His name was Samuel Danzinger and he worked as a chocolate salesman for my father in Radom before the war. It was such a tragedy because Samuel was lucky to survive the concentration camps and had just found his wife and child again.

The German police raid was a scary reminder that ignited a riot. "Just like Hitler, you come and make raids on Jews?!" We would never tolerate that! The whole DP camp, about 1,400 Jews, started marching through the city, screaming and yelling, demanding justice. I remember I was waving a colored flag. The protest was so strong that the U.S. Military Government ordered the German police to never ever go into the Stuttgart DP camp or any Jewish DP camp in Germany. The response to the German police raid in Stuttgart showed that Jews were ready to fight. Never again would Jews be sheep to the wolves.

In January, 1947, I walked to the Stuttgart train station to take a trip to visit some friends in Munich or Reitzberg. The building was half-demolished by Allied bombing, but the trains were running and the platform was crowded with travelers. Everyone was squeezed together, waiting for the train to come. Finally, we heard the toot of the engine and the train pulled into the station. The crowd pressed forward in a frenzied rush to get on board the train and secure a seat. I noticed two girls who were overwhelmed by the rough, surging mob. They were pinned against the side of the train, unable to move toward the doors. So I came to their rescue. I picked the first girl up and pushed her through one of the car windows. Then I lifted the second girl and did the same. Just like that, they were safely on board. One girl was a stunner, with dark eyes and thick, curly black hair. I was smitten. I scrambled through the window myself to talk to her. She was young, just sixteen, and extremely shy. She would not even speak to me! I kept trying to converse and she continued to ignore me, but I did manage to get her name—Goldie Cukier. Her last name means "sugar." How fabulous! Somewhere later in the trip, I lost sight of the two girls in another crowded train station.

I returned to Stuttgart, sad that I would never see Goldie again. At that point during our first year in Stuttgart, my whole family was planning to emigrate to Israel, so I wanted to be fluent in Hebrew. I found a friend of my father named Rosenberg who gave me a crash course in Hebrew. I learned it so well and so quickly that they asked me to teach Hebrew in the new Jewish school. I was the teacher, but I was not much older than the students! Some were a few years younger, some were my age. One day, about a month after the train station incident, a new student walked into my class. My heart jumped. It was Goldie!

She was still very shy, but now I had a new chance. Since we were all in the same age group, the students and I often socialized together after class. But it wasn't easy to win her. There were a dozen guys chasing after Goldie. Some richer, some smarter, some better-looking. But I kept pursuing her

It's funny, but I knew right away I was going to marry Goldie. Every day I would come home and tell my mother, "I'm going to marry the *shvartza maidel*" (the dark girl).

And my mother would reply, "Okay, so you're going to marry her. Bring her over here and let me meet her!"

That took a long time because Goldie was so shy. Eventually she agreed to go out with me. It wasn't long before I proposed marriage, too. But Goldie wouldn't say yes or no. So when I couldn't wait any longer, I went to see the couple who were like her adoptive parents—Frania (Frances) and Sam Zimmerman. They liked me. They said yes. Then Goldie said yes.

But I've been talking too much. It is time to meet Goldie and hear her story, too.

# Part II

## Goldie's Story

# Chapter Eight

## High Ceilings and Light

My name is Goldie Cukier Finkelstein. I was born on August 3, 1929, in the city of Haifa in Israel. My parents, Joseph Cukier and Miriam (Mania) Goldstein Cukier, had traveled from their home in Sosnowiec, Poland, to the Holy Land around 1925 after they lost their very first child. As a way of dealing with their grief, the young married couple went on a "grand tour" and ended up in Palestine, which was then under British control. They settled down in Haifa, a port city on the Mediterranean, and began a family. My oldest sister Tobka (we always called her Toby) was born there in 1926 and I was born three years later.

Shortly after my birth, my parents decided to return to their hometown of Sosnowiec, Poland. The reason is still unclear, but it was home to my four grandparents, Chaim and Gitel Cukier, and Simon and Chava Goldstein, and most of my other relatives. My father was the second of four children, with two brothers, Berel and Pinkus, and a sister Mania. My mother was one of six children, one brother Ateek, and four sisters, Gucia, Bruya, and two others whose names I don't recall. At that time, Sosnowiec was a thriving city of about 130,000 people, with a Jewish population of 28,000. It is located in the southern part of Poland in a region called Silesia.

My father became wealthy in Sosnowiec as a wholesale dry goods merchant and my parents had two more children: my brother Alter, who we called Ateek, and my baby sister Gucia. We enjoyed a privileged life before the war. My father's store was three stories tall and employed many people in Sosnowiec, both Jews and Gentiles. We were a prominent and well-respected family in the city. Our apartment at 10 Warszawska Street, near the grand train station, was large and luxurious with elegant moldings, tall windows, high ceilings and light.

The apartment entrance from the street was through a gateway which opened to the courtyard within. The front door, on the right of this gateway, opened onto a marble staircase with ornate metalwork, which led up to our apartment on the first level above the street, where there was a grand double door at the front entrance. Our rear door entered from the landscaped courtyard, up one flight of back stairs. The children and the maids always used the small back door to enter our apartment through the kitchen. Only our parents and their friends would use the front entrance.

Our family had our own live-in maid and full-time cook to help with the children and housework, so eight people lived comfortably in our large and elegant home. Hired help was also a necessity because my mother worked full-time in our dry goods store at 11 Modrzejowska Street, which was just around the corner from our home. The store was so close that I could easily go visit my parents whenever I wanted to.

We had a wonderful loving family. Everyone got along well. I felt good about myself. I remember one time that we were on vacation for the summer. I was maybe seven years old, standing and looking at myself in the mirror and my mother was standing behind me. I said, "Mom, I'm really beautiful."

"Yes, Goldie, you are," she said, "but that doesn't mean anything. It's what's inside you that counts. Beauty won't take you any place."

I never forgot what Mother said that day. I suppose that's why I never thought that I was really beautiful. Instead I focused more on developing my mind and abilities, especially in school. School was very important in our family because education was highly prized. My dream was to become a physician someday. A typical day would begin with breakfast, then we would walk to school and return home about 2 p.m. My parents would come home for dinner at 3 p.m., which was customary in Poland in those days. Then I would go to my Hebrew school, which was called *Beit Yaakov*. I also belonged to a Zionist youth group called *Hanoar*. I think I was actually a little too young to join, but I begged my older sister Toby to let me tag along, and they let me in.

The Jewish community was different than it is today in America. There was maybe one very large synagogue in Sosnowiec, but most Jews in our city belonged to little neighborhood prayer rooms called *shtiebeleh* where they gathered together for worship. Even on the big Jewish holidays, my entire family would go to the *shtiebeleh* rather than the large synagogue. My mother's father, Simon Goldstein, was so knowledgeable in Jewish law and Talmud that rabbis would seek out his advice. I remember that I had to always wear long sleeves when we visited my grandfather and grandmother Goldstein because it was immodest for a young Jewish woman to be uncovered.

Our household was not nearly as observant as Grandfather Goldstein. Still, my parents came home early every Friday afternoon for a traditional Sabbath evening celebration. My father and brother Ateek would go to the synagogue and return for *Shabbos* candles and dinner. Sometimes we had guests for the *Shabbos* dinner, which was a customary way to give charity. My father would invite *Yeshiva buchers*, students from the local Jewish academy, who had no place to go for the Sabbath meal. After dinner, we would sing the traditional Hebrew songs called *z'mirahs*.

In the summer we would escape the city for a long vacation. My parents would rent a house or a cottage in the mountains, where we stayed from the end of school in June until a few days before school began in September. My mother would stay with us, and Father would come on weekends. It was always lovely. In the summer of 1939, our last vacation before the war, we traveled farther than usual to a place in the mountains called Rajcza. We had to take a train and a bus to get there. This picture is one of only two photos that I have of my childhood. One of my friends gave it back to me after the war. I am ten years old and standing with my father's youngest brother, Uncle Pinkus.

Goldie Cukier, age 10, with her father's younger brother, Uncle Pinkus Cukier, on summer vacation in the countryside in 1939. Uncle Pinkus later died in the gas chambers at Auschwitz.

My life before the war was simple, happy, and carefree. I was pretty. I had many girlfriends. I only remember one sad moment before the war, my mother sitting *shiva* for her mother. It was the first time I ever saw my mother cry. Otherwise, I had no worries, not even the annoyance of anti-Semitism, which was extremely strong in Poland. Maybe I was more sheltered from the racial hatred because I was young and a girl and more well-to-do, but my first awareness of anti-Semitism was when I was nine years old. One Saturday night, in 1938, my parents came home from the theater where an *Endek* had intentionally burned a hole in a Jewish woman's fur coat. There was a great uproar in the theater over this act of racial hatred. Even though the Poles hated the Jews, it was shocking to see this level of outright hostility at a fancy theater. The *Endeks* were fascists who took their name from the initials of their political party, the National Democrats—ND or *Endek*—which was the equivalent of the Nazi party in Germany. As Nazi Germany became stronger and stronger in Europe and began to conquer more territories in 1938 and 1939, so too the *Endeks* became more and more brazen in harassing, terrorizing and beating Jews in Poland.

As a 10 year old in fifth grade, I was too young to comprehend the politics of what was happening in Europe that summer. Perhaps my parents knew that trouble was coming because we ended our country vacation just days before the Germans launched their invasion of Poland on September 1, 1939. The trains immediately began to run badly and we had great difficulty getting our vacation luggage back. By September 4, 1939, the German *blitzkrieg* had overrun Sosnowiec in pursuit of the retreating Polish Army. Being so young, I was actually happy about the war because I didn't have to go to school. I could stay home and play.

It did not take long for me to realize that this was a catastrophe. Within the first week, the Germans burned down the Great Synagogue on Dekert Street and began hitting and grabbing Jewish men off the street for forced labor. In some ways, the Germans treated the people in our border region a little better than other parts of Poland because they considered our area to be "*Reichsdeutschland*," a part of their ethnic homeland. Before World War I, the mostly Polish parts of Upper Silesia, along with the city of Sosnowiec, had belonged to Germany. Now they reclaimed it.

All in all, the first weeks and months of the German occupation were not too harsh. The Germans set up a Jewish Council, called the *Judenrat*, and Jewish police to enforce their rules against the Jews. Jews had to wear arm bands or yellow Jewish stars on their clothing that said "*Jude*" and the Germans requisitioned all Jewish businesses. If a Jew had a shop or factory, it had to have a German civilian "own" the business. One day, my father went to his dry goods warehouse and found a lock on the door with a sign that he had to have a German to operate his business.

We soon lost our live-in maid, too. Since she was born in Silesia, the Germans considered her to be *Volksdeutsche*, an ethnic German, and of course, a German could never work for Jews. But she loved our family and remained loyal, often bringing us food in the hard times to come. The cook, who was a Jewish orphan from a tiny Polish village, stayed with us. My mother had taken her in like a family member and later gave her away as a bride to a nice Jewish husband. I don't know what happened to her after she married and moved out.

In the beginning of the Occupation, the Germans opened schools that taught German instead of Polish as the native language. We had always spoken Polish except when my parents spoke Yiddish to keep something secret from us children. Now we had to learn German. But this did not last very long. My parents would not let us go to school because there were so many raids on the street and they were afraid that we might be captured and sent away to a forced labor camp. It was a frightening time. At any random moment, Germans could round people up, usually able-bodied Jewish men, but sometimes women too, and drag them away to who knows where. If a man was lucky, the work might be forced labor in the city, but usually the Germans would take the men away and they would never return.

One day, there was a knock on the door and a bedraggled Polish soldier walked in. At first we didn't recognize him. It was my cousin's husband, who had been released from a POW camp. I raced down the street to my cousin's house to tell her the good news that her husband was alive and bring her to see him. I still remember that incident. It must have been in early 1940.

Throughout the first year of the Occupation, the Germans continued to randomly grab people off the street for forced labor. We stayed inside as much as we could to avoid trouble. As a wealthy merchant, forced to operate his business for a German, my father used his money, influence and connections to get the *Judenrat* to allow us to remain in our nice apartment. But his wealth also made him a target. There were many times that the Gestapo would suddenly knock on our door, seize Father and take him away. Each time we feared that we would never see him again. The Germans would take him to the dry goods warehouse, pick out the merchandise they wanted, load it up and go. Eventually, there was a day in 1941 when a worker came running from the warehouse to tell Father that the Germans had emptied the entire store. In a single day, all the merchandise was loaded onto trucks and taken to Germany. After that, my parents stayed home.

Between the random raids on the street and the raids on our apartment, we were terrified that the Germans would seize Father. So we devised a plan. If the Germans knocked on the front door, we hid Father in the back of the apartment and pushed a big wardrobe against the door. Our apartment was so huge that no one would suspect that there were more rooms in the back. If the Germans knocked on the back door, we hid Father in the front rooms and pushed a wardrobe against the door on the other side. This is how we saved my father from being taken away.

But that did not stop the Germans from stealing our possessions. At any time they could march in and take the fine china or the silver or the crystal or the rugs, whatever they wanted. We could do nothing but give it to them and hope they would leave us alone. There were so many raids that we slept in our clothes. We never undressed because we never knew when the Germans would come to harass us.

Despite the worsening situation, my parents tried to give us an education and as normal of a life as possible. Since the Germans had forbidden all schooling for Jewish children, there were many Jewish professors and teachers who were out of work. My parents hired a few to give us private lessons at home. They taught us many subjects. One of the teachers was an Englishman. My parents insisted on giving us English lessons because Israel was under British rule. They still retained their passports from when we lived in Israel and my father pledged that, "No matter what, after the war is over, we're going back to Palestine. We're not going to stay in Poland." So I learned English. I couldn't converse in it, but I knew simple things like "this is a table" and "that is a pencil."

I was too young to know it at the time, but the history books say that the Germans first began deporting groups of sixty to seventy Jews from Sosnowiec to the gas chambers at Auschwitz in March, 1942. The first large deportation from Sosnowiec was in May, 1942, when 1,500 Jews, mostly the old and sick, were taken to the railway station and packed into cattle cars for Auschwitz. A month later, the Germans emptied the old-age home and orphanage and sent 2,000 more victims to the gas chambers.

Then, what was later called "the Great Deportation" began on August 12, 1942. It was a day I vividly remember. Every Jew in the city was ordered to assemble at a central square/transit camp in Sosnowiec. We were surrounded by SS troops and German police with machine guns. It was a long day of anxious waiting as thousands of frightened Jews were crowded together. We did not know it at the time, but this was a "*selektion.*" The Nazis were deciding who would live and who would die. Each family group would have to pass in front of the Germans and they would make their picks. They broke up many families, taking a father or mother or daughter or brother, whoever they wanted. My father's sister and her husband were among those taken away. It was such a tragedy and nobody knew where anyone was being taken. Today, we know from the historians that some were picked to stay in their jobs in Sosnowiec, about 3,000 were picked for deportation to other forced labor camps in Germany, and about 8,000, especially the children, elderly, and weak, were picked for the gas chambers at Auschwitz. The first 2,000 were sent to death on that first day and 6,000 more disappeared over the next five days.

We were one of the luckiest families because no one was separated, and we were released to return to our home that night. We were spared again, no doubt, because my father was well-to-do and he could use his money and influence with the Jewish men in power that had connections with the Germans. Two months after the Great Deportation, in October, 1942, the SS created a ghetto for the Jews of Sosnowiec in a suburb called Srodula. We were lucky. Father once again bribed the *Judenrat* to keep us in our own home.

Now it was more important than ever to have a job. Father knew that if you were working for a German company in Sosnowiec, it could protect you from being kidnapped off the street and sent away to some far-away work camp. We still had no knowledge of concentration camps, or extermination camps, only forced labor camps. So my father had arranged for my older sister Toby and me to get working papers and jobs in the city. As young as I was, just 12 or 13, my job was painting ceramic tiles for a German company. My sister Toby worked for the German Army, the *Wehrmacht*, manufacturing knapsacks. I think we both worked from 1942 to 1943. My parents could do nothing as far as work so they stayed in the apartment with my little brother and sister.

During this period, we were somewhat safe and could live together as a family. Food was more scarce, but we were not starving. We still had our apartment. We still had some money to live on. But it wasn't a happy life because we were constantly scared of raids. I remember that my sister and I would sneak out to attend meetings of *Hanoar*, a Zionist youth organization. Despite the danger of being caught after curfew, we would get together to sing Jewish songs and have fun.

Then disaster struck. In February or March, 1943, I was just walking down the street and the Germans grabbed me in a random raid. I was taken to the square in old Sosnowiec that served as the transit camp for processing and deporting Jews. An hour later, my sister Toby was caught in another raid and brought to the same place. My parents were very distraught when they found out. My father immediately tried to get the *Judenrat* to release us. The Nazis did not care which Jews they took—as long as their quota for workers was filled. At first, it looked like Father had succeeded because my sister and I were walking out of the gate to join him. Then an SS officer stopped us.

"What is this, two sisters?" he barked. "No. Only one may be released. One must stay. You must choose."

My father suddenly had to make an awful choice. We talked briefly. I was 13 years old and looked even younger, like a pre-teen girl, but Toby was a mature and beautiful young woman, so we thought she would be at greater risk. So I said to my older sister, "They aren't going to do anything to me, Toby, I'm too young. You go home."

Forced to choose on the spot, my father left with Toby. I'm sure Father believed that he could get me out very quickly, too. As they walked away, I never imagined that it would be the last time I saw them alive. I never had a chance to say goodbye to my family. And I never knew what happened to them until after the war.

My older sister Toby was 15 years old in this damaged photograph fragment that survived the war. She is wearing the yellow star "*Jude*" on her sweater. She died in 1943 at age 17 in the gas chambers at Auschwitz.

# CHAPTER NINE

# A Child Alone

A short time later, before my father could get me out of the Sosnowiec transit camp, I was pushed into a cattle car and deported to another transit camp in Poland called Gogolin. I was only there for a short time, but I was relieved to find a lot of my friends from Sosnowiec were there too. But none of them were sent to the same camp that I was. It was called Graeben (or Gräben). It was one of many subcamps of the main Gross-Rosen Concentration Camp about 170 miles northwest of Sosnowiec.

Graeben was a small female work camp with about 500 prisoners. I was a young girl alone, very naive and scared, so I did whatever anyone told me to do. I worked hard at any task I was given. I was fortunate because, as young as I was, I looked even younger. So the other prisoners considered me a child and tried to protect me.

Life was very structured at Graeben. We were awakened for roll call in the early morning; then we got a piece of bread or some thin soup; then we marched from the barracks to the factory; and finally, after a long day of work, we would return for another bowl of thin soup and go to sleep. The factory turned flax into fabric for military uniforms and flags. The raw flax would come out of a machine like spaghetti, which we would twist together into bales for baking. Then we would put the dry flax bales into the hot oven to create pieces of silky cloth. After that step, we would pack the pieces of cloth into a bale, which would be wrapped together with wire for shipping. The process involved a big machine, which would frequently break down. Many times I fixed the machine myself—with a crowbar. I don't know how I knew what to do, but I did it.

We worked all day long, seven days a week. Every day was like every other day. Just work, work, work. I had no idea of the days of the week or months of the year. In an odd way, I felt relief to be sent away from my family because I no longer had to worry about my father or my family and the next terrifying raid by the Germans. I only had to worry about me and nobody else. That doesn't mean that I forgot about my family. I often thought about them. I imagined them being safe at home and told myself that the war will be over soon and I'll see them again. I never thought for a minute that they were not going to survive. I naively believed I would be reunited with all of them after the war ended. It was this belief that kept me going.

It helped, of course, to hear some direct information about my family. A few weeks after I was deported, my sister Toby's best friend, Bella Jakubowicz,[5] was caught in another raid in Sosnowiec and also sent to Graeben. Bella told me how distraught my family was over my deportation, but that they were all still alive. For a few months, I was even getting letters and packages from home because Graeben was only a working camp, not an SS concentration camp yet. My parents sent me things like beautiful silk underwear, which I could use to trade for extra food. And my little sister Gucia, who was only nine years old, was writing letters to me in beautiful German Gothic script. Since all letters were inspected by the camp, there was a German woman who read every letter. She was thrilled that a little Jewish girl could write such beautiful German Gothic letters.

Then the letters stopped abruptly in the first days of August, 1943. I wondered why, and missed hearing from my family, but I did not imagine they were in any serious trouble.

I continued to work in the factory at Graeben through the summer and fall of 1943 and on into the fifth winter of the war. Then, some time around February, 1944, another disaster struck. The SS took control over Graeben from the German Army and turned it into a concentration camp. I'll never forget that day as long as I live. The SS ordered everyone outside. Then they ordered us to strip naked. Five hundred girls and women were shivering from the cold and shame. Can you imagine young girls and teenagers forced to strip naked in front of grown men? The bullies stood there and stared at us, grinning and laughing. It was humiliating and frightening. They examined every girl and woman, and if they saw anything physically wrong, they took her away for extermination.

When the Nazis took our clothes, they also confiscated any possessions we might have—jewelry, watches, books, family photographs. They stole our jewelry and anything of value and threw every photograph into a bonfire. I lost the few precious pictures of my family that I still had. But the Germans were still not finished with their cruelty. They mixed up all of our clothes as a joke, giving a tall woman's clothing to a short woman, a large girl's clothing to a small girl, and so on.

---

[5]    Bella Jakubowicz survived the war and married to become Bella Tovey. Her story is featured on the US Holocaust Museum website. It was Bella who saved the damaged photo of Toby and gave it to Goldie after the war.

That horrible day was just the beginning. Everything changed for the worse when the SS took over Graeben. The rules became stricter and the punishments more frequent and severe. The food rations were reduced to near-starvation levels. And the barracks were crowded with more prisoners. They forced three women into a wooden bunk that was not big enough for one. And the bunks were stacked three rows high so if someone in the upper bunk was sick or had diarrhea, the person below would suffer. There were so many incidents of abuse and misery that I tried to block it out of my mind. I remember a girl whose arm was caught in one of the machines and severely mangled. It was a gruesome bloody sight and the SS would show no mercy for any worker who could no longer work. It was a death sentence for that poor girl.

Today I remember very little from that period, just a few of the girls' names that I kept in touch with after the war. Otherwise I did not want to remember, and I don't remember today. I spoke fluent German in the camps because when we spoke to the Germans, we always had to speak German. Today I can't speak a word of German. It's like my mind has closed off the memories of those terrible years.

There was a particular German SS woman who I will always remember. She was in charge of the flax factory at Graeben. She fell in love with me because I was so young and cute. I don't recall her name, but she treated me like her sweet pet. She was a good-looking woman, who always covered her hair with a scarf for some reason, and she was always kind to me and frequently brought food to me in the factory. But this German SS woman was a terrible brute to everyone else in camp. If someone failed to do their job correctly, they received a severe beating from her or one of her *kapos*. I was so outraged by her brutality to my friends that I didn't want to talk to her. In my naïve sense of loyalty and honor, I refused any kindness or help from the SS woman. If I did accept food from her, I would save it and give it to the other hungry girls later.

As time passed, more girls from the Sosnowiec ghetto were captured in raids and sent to Graeben. Some were my childhood friends; others were people I knew from my hometown and neighborhood. In particular, there was a nurse who lived in the same building as my family. She had risen to a position of importance in the camp and took personal interest in protecting me. But I rejected her help also. It doesn't make any sense to me now, but I felt it was unfair to receive any special treatment when so many others were suffering so greatly.

One day, the SS brought a transport of girls from Auschwitz into our camp. We were shocked and horrified by their appearance. They all had shaved heads and wore striped uniforms. Even worse, they told us about the gas chambers and mass murder and crematoriums. It was the first time anyone had ever heard of Auschwitz and it was just too horrible to believe. Who could conceive of such a thing? I think most of the prisoners did not believe the girls from Auschwitz.

## I. Schicht (vom 15. bis 19.1.45)

| | | | | | | |
|---|---|---|---|---|---|---|
| 1. | Almer | Adela | 48006 | 27. | Honigmann | Hena | 48666 |
| 2. | Borter | Bajla | 35465 | 28. | Herszkowicz | Zosia | 51196 |
| 3. | Borowiecka | Blima | 48081 | 29. | Kilberg | Chaja | 48680 |
| 4. | Durantyn | Halina | 48027 | 30. | Kaufman | Bronka | 48695 |
| 5. | Bachner | Margot | 48807 | 31. | Kruk | Gerda | 48904 |
| 6. | Bajchlmocher | Pejla | 48808 | 32. | Klajnbaum | Marianne | 51237 |
| 7. | Bienenstock | Helene | 35465 | 33. | Lewi | Cyoora | 51264 |
| 8. | Biatka | Sala | 48913 | 34. | Lirowcka | Chana | 48715 |
| 9. | Ciesla | Dobra | 48850 | 35. | Oksenhandler | Anna | 48727 |
| 10. | Chorstan | Blima | 48029 | 36. | Przednowek | Pesla | 48834 |
| 11. | Eisenberg | Salomea | 48842 | 37. | Romankiewicz | Fejgla | 48844 |
| 12. | Achner | Toni | 48858 | 38. | Reichenbaum | Frieda | 48842 |
| 13. | Ebel | Adela | 35480 | 39. | Schwarzberg | Maria | 48875 |
| 14. | Frenkel | Ester | 48854 | 40. | Silberfeld | Jana | 48860 |
| 15. | Frucht | Tonia | 48859 | 41. | Szenker | Gusta | 48855 |
| 16. | Fer us | Sara | 48850 | 42. | Ulreich | Chawke | 48961 |
| 17. | Feldman | Gerda | 35492 | 43. | Ubersfeld | Szajndla | 48979 |
| 18. | Zielinska | Sala | 48798 | 44. | Ubersfeld | Chaja | 48980 |
| 19. | Frajdeniejch | G | 67250 | 45. | Weiss | Rosa | 48993 |
| 20. | Glass | Micha | 48365 | 46. | Wachsberg | Estera | 48902 |
| 21. | Gerszt | Machela | 51175 | 47. | Weinstein | Lola | 48775 |
| 22. | Gerszt | Sura | 51174 | 48. | Warszawska | Frieda | 48987 |
| 23. | Herszthal | Tosia | 48882 | 49. | Weissman | Priwa | 48994 |
| 24. | Heller | Franciszka | 48660 | 50. | Weis | Ewa | 53992 |
| 25. | Haftel | Rosalie | 48878 | 51. | Weis | Rywka | 53923 |
| 26. | Himmelfarb | Gusta | 48883 | 52. | Reifer | Ruchla | 48754 |

## II. Schicht (vom 15. bis 19.1.45)

| | | | | | | |
|---|---|---|---|---|---|---|
| 1. | Adler | E Ester | 35456 | 27. | Mangel | Ruchla | 48708 |
| 2. | Bajtner | Rywka | 38458 | 28. | Muszkatenblum | Ester | 48719 |
| 3. | Borger | Ester | 48521 | 29. | Jajfeld | Franka | 48720 |
| 4. | Borger | Pegza | 35471 | 30. | Michthauser | Felicie | 48725 |
| 5. | Bornstein | Chanie | 35470 | 31. | Feugewirtz | Fela | 48724 |
| 6. | Bornstein | Sala | 35469 | 32. | Pipersberg | Hermina | 48729 |
| 7. | Bornstein | Chaja | 48820 | 33. | Pergament | Fajga | 51283 |
| 8. | Birner | Elli | 35478 | 34. | Pergament | Lana | 51262 |
| 9. | Cukier | Golda | 35475 | 35. | Rotter | Ida | 48733 |
| 10. | Rottenberg | Sonia | 52118 | 36. | Rotter | Ilza | 48739 |
| 11. | Edelstein | Rosalie | 35461 | 37. | Rosenberg | Chaja | 48846 |
| 12. | Friedman | Chaja | 55497 | 38. | Schwarz | Ita | 48752 |
| 13. | Frisch | Mirla | 48853 | 39. | Sternlicht | Olga | 48770 |
| 14. | Gromer | Eugenia | 48651 | 40. | Sworzynska | Adela | 55995 |
| 15. | Gellkopf | Rojza | 35500 | 41. | Wachsman | Blima | 48766 |
| 16. | Gross | Gusta | 48871 | 42. | Wekselman | Mirla | 56288 |
| 17. | Hornung | Frieda | 48668 | 43. | Wodzistawska | Gitla | 48999 |
| 18. | Hauptschein | Mina | 48379 | 44. | Wittler | Kojla | 48779 |
| 19. | Hofman | Chaja | 48884 | 45. | Wajndling | Bajla | 48770 |
| 20. | Jucker | Cilla | 48672 | 46. | Taus | Adela | 48751 |
| 21. | Korn | Rosalie | 48692 | 47. | Tendler | Hinda | 48756 |
| 22. | Klajman | Gitla | 48656 | 48. | Trzcinka | Ala | 55018 |
| 23. | Knoblauch | Chanka | 48688 | 49. | Zylbernik | Uaja | 48702 |
| 24. | Lehrfeld | Helena | 48700 | 50. | Zaks | Frajdla | 48744 |
| 25. | Weser | Szajndla | 48701 | 51. | Zellerkaut | Dola | 50305 |
| 26. | Kiwkowicz | Chana | 48683 | 52. | Silberberg | Est | 53939 |

This document is a Nazi record of forced laborers in Graeben concentration camp. It shows two shifts of 52 female slave laborers working at Graeben for the period of January 15 to 19, 1945. Goldie is listed ninth in the second group as "Golda Cukier," prisoner #35475.

More time passed. A second winter came to Graeben. We continued to endure. The rules were very strict, but I always worked hard and behaved politely so that nobody would bother me. I escaped any beatings except for one time, when a German woman in the factory was inspecting our work and slapped me. This happened in the final days at the camp in January, 1945. By then, I had been a prisoner in Graeben camp for nearly two years and we were hearing rumors that the Russian Army was coming closer. We dared to hope that the Russians might save us.

But then, one day in late January or early February, 1945, the German SS woman in charge of the factory approached me. "You know," she said kindly, "they are going to close the camp tonight and send you all away. I want you to come with me. I want to hide you." She actually wanted to adopt me as her child, which is unbelievably strange because she was a Nazi and I was a Jewish teenage girl.

I listened to her offer, then proudly refused. "No," I replied, "I'm not going anywhere with a German. Leave me alone. I'll go with the others." The SS woman tried to save me from the death march to come, but I was stubborn. I would not go with her.

Sure enough, the SS suddenly evacuated the Graeben concentration camp in the middle of the night. The Germans woke everyone up, ordered us to get dressed, and drove us outside into the freezing darkness. The Germans said that we had to move the whole camp. They took our normal shoes and replaced them with wooden clogs and gave us workers jeans. We obeyed every order like cattle and marched out of the camp in columns.

Tramping in the darkness, we had no idea where we were going or what lay ahead. We had no coats for the winter cold and had to walk through deep snow in those awful wooden clogs. No one dared to stop and rest because the SS men would shoot you. We walked and walked and walked—always on the side of the road—for three long terrible days. Many women were too weak to keep going and collapsed. Many died on the road and their bodies were left where they fell. The death march was a hellish thing, but I don't remember much because my mind was focused only on survival—keep marching, keep marching, don't stop, keep marching.

Eventually we reached a place where they loaded the survivors of the death march onto a long train with closed and open cattle cars. We could see the heads of thousands of male prisoners who were already on the same train, freezing and starving in the open cars. They loaded our group of female prisoners into two or three of the open cattle cars. We had no idea where the train was going, but we were thankful, finally, to stop marching.

# CHAPTER TEN

## Babylon

The train traveled for several days. It was February and we were freezing in the open cattle cars. Everyone was cold and hungry. During the ride, an SS guard offered me bread. I was surprised. The SS would never share their own food with a Jew. I suppose he was kind to me because of my child's face and thick curly hair. I accepted the bread, but did not eat because I saved it to share with others later.

There was one time that the cattle train stopped for a short rest. I walked through the snow to a frozen lake, where I stripped and washed myself in the icy water. It was frigid cold, but I knew it was important to try to keep myself clean. Then we got back on the train. Many prisoners died on that trip from starvation and exposure to the severe cold, but the SS would not allow us to remove the corpses because it would leave evidence of their atrocities.

Finally, in the darkness of night, the train arrived at a large concentration camp. All we could see was a tall chimney belching smoke. Our hearts fell as we remembered the stories of the girls from Auschwitz. Surely this was the crematorium and we were all going to the gas chambers. The SS guards, who were both men and women, started shouting "*Raus, raus!*" (Out! Out!). They used big German shepherds that barked and snapped to drive the frightened prisoners from the cattle cars and march us in columns through the darkness into the camp.

Our group of girls and women entered a big hall. There were female *kapos*, who told us that this was Bergen-Belsen Concentration Camp, not Auschwitz. We did not believe them. We thought we were going to the gas chambers because the SS told us to strip off our clothes and enter the shower room. The SS claimed that they would delouse our clothes and give them back after the shower. And there were women with clippers who were shaving the hair from the women and girls. I was just a terrified child of fifteen, overwhelmed by the noise and confusion.

Then I heard someone call my name in Polish.

"Goldya!" I turned around. It was an older woman named Mania Sendiszew whose father had a dairy restaurant in the same building in Sosnowiec where my father had his store. She was assigned to work in this area and recognized me and called me over. "Goldya, give me your clothes," she explained, "I'm going to put them on the side so that when you come out, you'll get your own clothes back." I also had a silver watch that I had somehow saved. She took the watch for safekeeping and escorted me past the women with clippers so that they would not shave my hair off. I still had my long, beautiful, black hair.

I went into the shower with the other women and girls. When we came out, they gave us clothes. Again, everyone's clothes were mixed up. I was the lucky one. Just as she promised, Mania returned my clothes, along with the silver watch.

The *kapos* then pushed our large group into an enormous barrack. There were no bunks or beds so thousands of women were jammed together in tight rows across the floor. You couldn't walk without stepping on people. It was the most horrible place I've ever seen, filthy, smelly and crowded. It was unimaginable. It was Babylon.

I stayed in that hideous barrack for a week while the Germans were assigning jobs to the new prisoners. One day, two Czech *kapos* came in and said they needed five girls for the *Bewachungsturm*, which means guard tower or watchtower. They looked us over and chose me because I still had my long hair and I looked like a pretty, relatively healthy, girl. I was fifteen, but looked so much younger and innocent that I was no threat to anybody. I was one of five girls chosen, including a girl named Sabina from a small town in Poland. The two *kapos* led us from the main camp at Bergen-Belsen to a separate small camp with older women, who did the cooking, laundry and housekeeping for the German SS guards in the watchtowers. There was even a Jewish orphanage in this subcamp, which the Nazis had used to prove their "good" care of the prisoners to the International Red Cross.

It was a great stroke of luck to be assigned to the watchtower subcamp because we were kept separate from the typhus epidemic that was killing thousands of prisoners in the main camp. The Germans had set up this separate camp and barracks to protect themselves from lice and infection. Our job was to take care of the rest quarters where the SS guards would eat their meals and nap in bunks between work shifts. The guards did not live there. We would change the bed sheets, scrub the floors, clean the latrines and keep the quarters tidy.

Amazingly, the German guards in the watchtower quarters did not act brutally toward the female prisoners. No one was ever beaten or cursed, or hurt in any way. In fact, the Germans were extra nice to me. They called me their "Little Gypsy" because of my long black hair, dark complexion and brown eyes, and treated me like a beloved pet.

Sometimes the girl prisoners were sent to the Jewish orphanage to get milk or supplies. One day, one of the *kapos* brought me there. I walked in and there was a commotion. Someone said something about "Dr. Bimko" and a moment later, a woman walked in. She looked at me and asked, "Are you Golda Cukier from Sosnowiec?"

"Yes," I replied.

"I am a good friend of your mother, Mania," she said with a smile. Her name was Dr. Hadassah Bimko. She had been a dentist before the war, and now she was the Jewish doctor in charge of the 150 Jewish children in the orphanage. Any kind of doctor became a medical doctor in the concentration camps. "If you need anything, Golda," Dr. Bimko said, "just let me know."

"Thank you, but I don't need anything," I said. "I'm fine. I'm fine." Once again, I was too proud to accept any special treatment if others were suffering.

"All right," Dr. Bimko insisted, "but if there's anything I can do for you, just let me know."

I went on my way. Instead of accepting any help, I tried to help others. There were women prisoners who walked by the watchtower each day to chop wood in the nearby forest. They looked miserable and I felt sorry for them. Since I was getting plenty of food in the watchtower camp, I stole food to give to the starving prisoners. When the wood choppers walked past each day, I would sneak over to the fence to give them food.

Unfortunately, I must have touched one of the wood choppers because I contracted both typhus and dysentery. This was in very late March or early April, 1945. The double illness struck me hard and fast. Soon I was too sick to even sit up. By then, typhus and dysentery were raging out of control in the main Bergen-Belsen camp, killing thousands of people who were already half-dead from starvation and exhaustion. On top of that, the SS poisoned the water supply before they abandoned the camp and ran away to escape arrest for war crimes.

On April 15, 1945, the first British tanks liberated the prisoners of Bergen-Belsen. It was the first day of Passover, the Jewish holiday of liberation from slavery, but I was so delirious with sickness that I wasn't even aware of our liberation. I was in a deadly situation because typhus makes you extremely thirsty, while drinking bad water causes dysentery and severe diarrhea. I had drunk the poisoned water.

I surely would have died there in the barracks except for Sabina, one of the five girls picked for the watchtower. Sabina saw my desperate condition and physically carried me to the camp hospital. By then, the hospital was overflowing with dying prisoners who looked like skeletons. They said that every bed was filled and they could not take any more admissions. But Sabina did not give up. She went directly to Dr. Bimko to plead for my life. As soon as Dr. Bimko heard my name, she immediately admitted me to the hospital. She put me in the top bed of a double bunk because the bottom patient was in danger of falling excrement if the person in the top bunk had dysentery. Dr. Bimko made sure that I received the best care possible, giving me medicine and feeding me milk, juice, and sterile water. She saved my life.

# Chapter Eleven

## Displaced Person

In the days and weeks that followed liberation, tens of thousands of people at Bergen-Belsen continued to die from the diseases, exhaustion and starvation, often because they tried to eat too much food too soon. In fact, nearly a third of the 60,000 prisoners at Bergen-Belsen died after liberation. Once again, I was one of the lucky ones because I was recovering in a hospital bed under the personal care of Dr. Bimko.[6] By then, I had dropped to barely 80 pounds.

I also had the added benefit of two nurses, sisters from Sosnowiec and both single, who knew me and took special care of me. The first sister, Andzia Kiwkowicz, lived in the same building as my family before the war and was sent to Graeben camp. The other sister, Hella Kiwkowicz, was one of the young women with shaved heads who came to Graeben from Auschwitz. Both sisters had been nurses at the Sosnowiec Jewish Hospital before the war and now they were assigned as nurses to the Bergen-Belsen hospital. Given my youth and our previous bond, the two sisters adopted me. They literally nursed me back to health and were like parents to me. Even after I was healthy, the sisters would not let me go live in the regular barracks in the Displaced Persons camp that

---

[6]   After liberation, Hadassah Bimko married Josef Rosensaft, the Chairman of the Jewish Committee, who was in charge of the Bergen-Belsen Displaced Persons Camp. Hadassah Bimko Rosensaft was credited with saving the lives of hundreds of Jewish inmates while at Auschwitz and for saving all but one of the 150 Jewish children in her care at the Bergen-Belsen orphanage. Dr. Bimko also played a major role as an eyewitness for the prosecution of Nazi war criminals in a British military court in Luneburg, Germany in 1945. She died in 1997 at the age of 85.

was created at Bergen-Belsen. They insisted that I continue living with them. They had their own separate nurse's quarters inside the hospital.

At one point, the Swedish Red Cross came to Bergen-Belsen and took a lot of orphaned girls to live in Sweden. They wanted to take me also, but the sisters refused to let me go. "You're staying with us," they insisted. So I did. It was a nice situation. Since I lived in the hospital, I would help with bandages and errands. I enjoyed this work so much that I wanted to become a doctor myself.

A short time later, a third sister came to join us at the Bergen Belsen hospital. Her name was Frania (Frances) Zimmerman and she had been the head nurse of the Jewish hospital in Sosnowiec before the war. She was the sister of Hella and Andzia Kiwkowicz. She also lived in my same apartment building before the war and knew my parents well. Frania, who was in her 30's at that time, had married during the war, but then was separated from her husband, whose name was Zrilek (Sam). Fortunately, he survived and they were happily reunited there at Bergen-Belsen. Sam and Frania and her two sisters, Hella and Andzia, became my new adopted family. We lived together happily, first in the hospital with the three sisters, and then later in an apartment with just Frania, Sam and me. Frania and Sam became my foster parents.

Still, as much as it was nice to be adopted, my heart ached for my real family, Father, Mother, Toby, Ateek and Gucia. I had believed that we would be reunited the moment the war was over. It was a belief that kept me going from the day I was separated in March, 1943, and it carried me through my darkest days in Graeben and Bergen-Belsen concentration camps.

I desperately wanted to find my family again. I wanted to go back to Poland to look for them, but Frania refused to let me go. She warned that it would not be safe for a pretty, innocent girl to go traveling alone through the Russian occupied zone. "If the Russians see a pretty girl like you," Frania warned, "they'll never let you go." I gave in, but I continued searching anywhere I could. When I found that my father's friend was in charge of the Jewish Committee in Sosnowiec, I wrote to him. I wrote letters to him for many months, but he always wrote back to say that he had heard nothing about my family. I followed every lead, good or bad. Once I received a letter from someone with the same name as my sister Toby. But it was a disappointment. My sister was well educated and had fine handwriting, but the letter had the words and handwriting of a child.

I was constantly looking for news. At night I had recurring dreams of walking into a room and finding my father and mother. "Where were you?" I would rebuke them in the dream. "How come I couldn't find you?!" It brings me to tears even now.

Gradually, I came to accept that everyone had perished. Not just my immediate family, but my grandparents, aunts, uncles, cousins, more than 40 close relatives, and most of my friends, too. I was the only survivor, a 15-year-old orphan. I remember saying to myself, "I never will get married. I never want to fall in love. I don't want to love anybody and lose them. I'm not going to have kids, because I couldn't bear the pain of losing anyone else that I love." That was my attitude for a long time. I was grieving, but I'm sure that others were more psychologically damaged than me, especially older people who were parents because there couldn't be anything worse than a mother losing her child.

After the war, I spoke to a friend who was still in Sosnowiec in August, 1943. She said that my family was deported on the last big transport from Sosnowiec to Auschwitz. I didn't know the exact date, but I knew it happened in early August because this was when the letters and packages stopped. It may have been August 16, 1943 because the history books show that the Sosnowiec ghetto was liquidated between August 1-16, 1943. During those two weeks, a total of 15,000 Jews were sent from Sosnowiec to the gas chambers at Auschwitz, including my dear family—Father, Mother, Toby, 17, Ateek, 12, and little 9 year-old Gucia—and my remaining aunts, uncles, cousins, and other extended family and relatives. God bless their memory.

There is a tiny possibility that Gucia was not with my parents in Auschwitz and could have survived the war as a hidden child. There was some talk that a Polish Christian woman in Sosnowiec, who was childless, was willing to take Gucia and raise her as her own child. I will never know if this plan took place. If so, Gucia might be alive today in Poland. But whatever happened, Gucia and the rest of my immediate and expanded family were lost to me forever. Because my father was forced to choose Toby and leave me behind, I was the sole survivor of my entire family.

All that I could do was try to start a new life. I had my new adoptive family and I made a lot of friends with girls from my old hometown, and girls who had been with me in the concentration camps. At that time, there were many survivors moving from DP camp to DP camp, searching for family and loved ones. I think many survivors were very sad on the inside, but most survivors were young people, glad to be alive. We made deep friendships. We got together for events and sang Hebrew songs. Many fell in love. And we took a lot of photographs! When I think about it now, I think we took so many pictures because we didn't have any. Our past lives were gone. We needed new pictures to mark our new lives.

We formed lasting friendships in the DP camp. Eventually, we dispersed all over the world—to Israel, Canada, Argentina and the United States. I stayed in contact with quite of few of them over the next 60 years. This picture shows two friends I made in Bergen-Belsen. It was taken in Stuttgart. I'm on the left. Bina Lederman is in the center. She was a schoolmate from Sosnowiec and we met again after the war. Her married name is Bina Peer. The other girl is Mila; I don't remember her last name. Bina and Mila are in Israel.

Goldie (on left) and two lasting friends from the DP camp:

Some survivors were angry and bitter after the war. They hated the Germans. I don't know how I had the wisdom as a young person, but I decided that I would not spend my life hating the Germans—because if I did, it would mean that the Germans won. "No," I said to myself, "I'm going to throw the hate out of my heart and I'm going to go on with my life." And this is what helped me. I know some survivors who were so full of hate that they passed it on to their own children and it just caused more misery.

One day a group of English soldiers came to see me. They had been searching for anyone who knew English to be a translator. My friends in camp remembered that I had been tutored in English and told the soldiers about me. I knew very little, of course, just a few words and a little grammar, but the British soldiers were thrilled to talk with anyone who knew English. It was fun.

Eventually, in the beginning of 1946, Sam and Frania and her two sisters decided to move to another Displaced Persons camp in Stuttgart, Germany. I went with them of course. They picked Stuttgart because Sam had two sisters and two brothers who survived the war and the brothers had started their own dentistry practice in Stuttgart. One dentist brother, Karl Zimmerman, gave me a job where I could be trained as a dental assistant. Suddenly, I had a medical career. And I also had the opportunity to go to high school in Stuttgart. It was called Beit Bialik and I loved it.

I lived with Sam and Frania in Stuttgart and we had a happy life. We did not actually live in the Displaced Persons camp, but outside in a nearby apartment. Most of my time was spent going to school and working as a dental assistant.

One day in early 1947, my friend Hella Kiwkowicz and I learned about another friend, who was being treated in a sanatorium for tuberculosis, and we decided to go visit. A lot of survivors had TB, and other sicknesses after the war. So we walked to the Stuttgart train station. At that time, trains were the only way you could travel, but the railroads were in ruin in Germany from bombing. Every train was so packed with people that it was a miracle to get aboard. When my girl friend and I tried to get on, all the doors were blocked with people. We were trapped in the crowd, unable to move. Suddenly a dapper young German man appeared. He was blond with green-blue eyes and wore a Tyrolean hat, brown leather jacket and brown leather boots. He spoke to us in German and offered his help. We agreed. Suddenly, he physically picked me up and pushed me through a window onto the train. He did the same for my friend Hella, and then climbed through the window himself.

I soon regretted taking his help because the stranger tried to flirt with us. I was a very shy, inexperienced girl, now just sixteen, and knew nothing of men. I was so innocent I thought you could get pregnant if a boy kisses you. And I sure did not want anything to do with any German! I wouldn't look at him. I tried to ignore him. I even said, "Please leave me alone." He was brash and persisted, but finally he gave up and went away.

I never imagined I would see the stranger again. But then, a few months later, I saw him on the streets of Stuttgart. I crossed the street to avoid him. It didn't work. He came after me and pursued me at every chance. His name was Sol Finkelstein. I was surprised to discover he was Jewish, not German, but I still did not want anything to do with him.

He wasn't the only boy who chased after me. There were other suitors, but I wasn't interested in any of them. I'm not boasting, but many of the young men in Stuttgart chased after me because I was pretty. One good-looking fellow was a cantor, who was madly in love with me. But I didn't like him. I had to change my walking route to work just so I wouldn't pass his window where he could see me.

In fact, I was often pestered by boys at the dental office where I worked. The office was on the street level so the boys would come look at me through the window. They would lie to the dentist, "Oh, I have a toothache," just so they could get to me!

Sol Finkelstein did that, too. He made such a nuisance out of himself that it was hard to avoid him. Then one day I went to take a Hebrew class at my high school. And there he was again! Sol turned out to be the Hebrew teacher. There was no way to avoid him now.

Goldie Cukier, age 17, at the Stuttgart Displaced Persons Camp in 1946.

# CHAPTER TWELVE

## "Pick Up" Girl

I did not want to have anything to do with Sol for a long time. I did not want to get close to anyone. But I saw him frequently because he was my teacher and our class group spent time together. Sol dressed like a *halutz*—a Jewish Zionist radical—in his leather boots, jacket and hat. He was outgoing and always singing popular songs, especially *Don't Fence Me In*. He was quite a character. Slowly, I warmed up to him, and agreed to date him, and very slowly, he became my very close friend. When Sol asked me to marry him, I hesitated because, like I said, I was afraid to fall in love and risk the pain of losing a loved one. So I couldn't accept. And I had my heart set on something else—Israel!

Many of us wanted to go to Israel. There was a big hall in Stuttgart where we all got together, and HIAS (Hebrew Immigrant Aid Society) would organize events. There was one man, in particular, who came from Israel. He thrilled us with stories of life in Israel and taught us to sing Hebrew songs. He was very influential in convincing young people to go to Israel, including many of my friends and me. That's why I wanted to go to Israel if I could. The problem was that it was illegal. At that time, the British ruled Palestine and, for political reasons, were blocking the immigration of any more Jews from Europe. In the summer of 1947, we learned of a secret ship that was leaving for Israel. A lot of my friends signed on, and I did too. I was all set to go. I even had a fake passport that some woman gave me. The photograph did not even look like me, but I didn't care. I was determined to go.

Then, on the night of the departure, Frania found out about the plan. To stop me, Frania and Sam took away my suitcase and all of my clothes, locked me in a room, and refused to let me out. "No," they said, "You are not going on a ship to Palestine. You are staying right here and marrying that man!"

I fussed and cried, but they would not let me out until the transport was gone. I was very distraught because all my friends were gone and I desperately wanted to go, too.

Ironically, the illegal transport turned out to be the famous ship *Exodus*. On July 11, 1947, the *Exodus* set sail from France with 4,500 refugees from various Displaced Persons camps in occupied Germany. But when the ship arrived in Israel, the British Royal Navy fired on the ship, killing three people, wounding dozens and damaging the boat. Eventually everyone on board was deported back to France, and then all the way back to Germany. It was an international news event and the *Exodus* became a symbol of the Zionist struggle for a Jewish state. The story later became a famous book and popular movie.

Of course, I did not know this at the time. Nor did I know that it was a blessing that Frania and Sam stopped me. Nearly the same thing happened to Sol's brother Joseph. Before I met Sol, his family had also planned to emigrate to Israel. They decided to send Joe ahead to find passage. Joe traveled all the way to Italy because that was the best way to find a ship that could get to Israel. But the British were doing everything they could to stop Jews from entering Palestine. The Italian ports were guarded and emigration became extremely difficult. So Joe was stuck in Italy. But it worked out nicely because he met and fell in love with a Jewish girl, who was also trying to get to Israel. Her name was Helen Mendelson and she came from the Transylvanian area of Hungary that borders Romania. Joe married Helen in Italy and brought her back to Stuttgart.

Meanwhile, Sol's sister Ann also fell in love, and married a man she met in Stuttgart. He was a Jewish fellow from Warsaw named Norbert (Natek) Berman, who was a medical student before the war. He had an uncle, Marcus Berman, who lived in New York City. When Uncle Marcus learned that Norbert was the only surviving member of the family, he insisted that they come and live in the United States. So Norbert and Ann applied for immigration papers.

Of course, Sol's mother was very close to Ann, especially after surviving the concentration camps together, and she was determined to keep the family together. So Sol's mother decided that the whole Finkelstein family would follow Ann and Norbert to the United States. Sol reluctantly agreed to go. Then he came to tell me the news.

"Goldie, you have to answer me," he said to me. "My mother is making papers for us to go to America. I have to know if you'll marry me. Otherwise if we don't make papers for you, you won't be able to go. I can't sleep and I can't eat. Marry me."

I looked at Sol. "Yes," I said, "I will marry you." I was in love with him.

We were married a few months later on Monday, November 17, 1947—the same day that Queen Elizabeth married Prince Philip. There was a nice restaurant in Stuttgart that was closed to the public on Mondays so we rented it for our wedding. I wore my white gown and Frania and Sam Zimmerman acted as my parents to escort me to the *chupah*, the wedding canopy. I was just eighteen years old. Sol was twenty two.

There are only a few photographs of the event, which were taken at home before the wedding. Unfortunately, the photographer never made it to our wedding because there was a snowstorm that day. Still, over one hundred guests came to our reception. It was lovely. Ann, Helen and Frania prepared a feast of gefilte fish and brisket and everyone danced to the wonderful orchestra. Later, we opened the wedding gifts. One gift was brought all the way from France by Ann's husband's best friend, Lew Levitan. It was a luxurious satin negligee. I turned red as a beet!

Goldie, age 18, on her wedding day, November 17, 1947.

Today we have a joke. When people ask how Sol and I met, Sol says, "She was a pick up girl"—because he physically picked me up and pushed me into the window of the train!

Goldie wrote the following words to Frania Zimmerman on the back of the picture to the left: " . . . so you'll remember me forever after I go to America."

The young couple sharing a happy moment in Stuttgart, 1947.

After I married Sol, we lived with his mother, his brother Joe and his wife Helen, and his sister Ann and her husband Norbert. His mother was a wise woman so she knew it would be awkward to live with her three adult married children. But my mother-in-law didn't want to live alone either. She came up with a solution. She re-married a religious Jew from Lodz named Yisrool (Israel) Farba, who had also lost his spouse in the concentration camps. He was a camp survivor himself and the match turned out very well.

So, now that everyone in the family was married, we lived communally in Stuttgart. Sol's mother, sister, and Helen did the cooking, while Sol, Joe and Norbert worked deals in the black market. All in all, it was a beautiful time. We were starting new lives and looking forward to having children and moving to America. We shared family dinners and spent every Shabbat together. This picture shows how we would often squeeze around the little dining room table to enjoy the Shabbat meal. This particular occasion was a wedding celebration for Sol's cousin Mary Korman from his hometown of Radom. Mary had just married Lew Levitan, who was Norbert's best friend and the Director of the Stuttgart DP camp. They later moved to Detroit.

From left to right: Goldie and Sol Finkelstein; Helen and Joe Finkelstein, stepfather Yisrool Farba and Sol's mother Golda; Sol's cousin Mary Korman and her husband Lew Levitan; and Ann Finkelstein Berman and Norbert Berman.

Here's another photo from Stuttgart that shows Norbert and Ann, Sol's mother, and Sol and myself. The skinny fellow in the black leather hat is Sol. This is how we looked when we lived in the Stuttgart DP camp.

From left to right: Norbert Berman and Ann Finkelstein Berman; Sol's mother, Golda Finkelstein Farba; and Sol and Goldie Finkelstein in the Stuttgart Displaced Persons Camp in 1947.

# CHAPTER THIRTEEN

## America

Nearly one year after our marriage, Sol and I boarded a boat for America with his brother Joe and Helen. All of the arrangements were done through HIAS and Norbert's uncle sponsored us. I was already five-months pregnant but we kept it a secret in case they wouldn't let me travel. The day we departed was November 8, 1948. The ship was a former military transport called the *U.S.S. General Omar Bundy*. It left Bremerhaven, Germany, with about 800 Displaced Persons as passengers. The men's and women's quarters were separated, so I was with Helen, and Sol was with Joe (Sol's sister Ann had already gone ahead with her husband Norbert to start a home in New York City.) We were all crowded in the lower decks of the ship in big, stuffy rooms with hundreds of other immigrants. Without windows or fresh air, nearly everyone was seasick.

I was so nauseous that they sent me to the doctor in the sick bay. I had removed my jewelry, and my wedding ring, which was loose on my finger, because it might have gotten lost or stolen. After examining me, the doctor frowned. Since I wore no wedding ring and looked very young, the doctor assumed that I was a promiscuous girl who had gotten pregnant out of wedlock. "Child, you are not married," he said angrily. "Do you know that you are pregnant?!"

"Doctor, I *am* a married woman," I said. I explained that my husband was down below with the men, why I was not wearing my wedding ring, and why I concealed my pregnancy.

As he listened, the doctor's expression changed. He was very kind. He ordered that I be moved from steerage to a private, first-class room above deck for the rest of the voyage. Now that was luxury! The doctor even allowed Helen to move up and share the room with me. But Sol and Joe had to stay below decks with the men.

From left: Sister-in-law Helen Finkelstein, Sol, Goldie and unknown friend on board the *U.S.S. General Omar Bundy* on arrival in Boston, November 18, 1948.

We landed in Boston on November 18, 1948. The ship was greeted by newspapers and fanfare because we were the first group from the 100,000 displaced persons who were permitted to immigrate to America outside of the quotas because of the Truman Act. It was exciting. Then we boarded a train for New York City. The Red Cross gave us juice and doughnuts on the way, and we all thought that America must be a wonderful place because they serve you food and drink for free!

Manhattan was so noisy and crowded. We found a little walk-up apartment in the lower, lower, lower East Side. For New Yorkers, that means we lived on Avenue C at 7th, which is as low on the East Side as you can get except for Delancey.

It felt strange to be new immigrants in America. Even the Jewish population looked at us funny. They lumped us all together like we were all the same. We had no face. A few of them dared to ask about the concentration camps.

"What did you do wrong?" somebody would ask. "Why would they incarcerate you if you didn't do anything? You must have done something bad to be put in a camp?!"

I couldn't believe that intelligent grown people could ask such questions. "No," I said, "We didn't do anything wrong."

Then somebody would ask, "You are such a young pretty girl. Didn't you get raped?"

"No," I replied, "Not everybody was raped."

One person even asked me, "Do you know what a banana is? Do you know what a car is?"

"I didn't grow up in Madagascar," I said. "I grew up in Europe. Europe was just as beautiful and modern as America."

You can imagine, after hearing such things, who would want to talk about the war or what we went through? I sure didn't.

My first son was born in March, 1949, at Beth Israel Hospital at 2nd Avenue and 18th Street. We named him Jacob Noah Finkelstein, after Sol's father. It was such a blessing. We continued living in the little walk-up apartment on the Lower East Side. It was hard to carry the baby and the baby carriage up and down the stairs. It wasn't so nice either that the neighborhood was dirty, and Sol was trying different jobs, but we managed. But the best thing was that we had close family. Every weekend we would take turns making dinner. I did Fridays, Helen did Saturdays, and Ann did Sundays. Later, in 1949, Sol's mother came to America and we would go to her house too.

That was our life in New York City. I suppose we all expected to live there permanently, but then Sol and his brother made a trip to South Jersey. When Sol came home, he announced that they bought two bungalows and we were moving to New Jersey to become chicken farmers! That was it. There was no discussion. I was just 20 years old with an eighteen-month-old baby. When my husband said I should go, I went. So, in August, 1950, we packed our things and baby Jacob into a cheap second-hand car and off we went to Vineland.

I had no idea what to expect. When I first saw the place, I almost fainted. It was just two little wooden houses in middle of the woods. There were no people, no houses, no street lights, no signs, no civilization, just forest and open fields. I was terrified. I came from a fairly big city and we only went to the country for summer vacations. This was the wilderness. Two bungalows in the middle of nowhere. I never lived in a little wooden house. I grew up in a huge, modern apartment building. "Do people really live here all year round in these little wooden houses?"

It was even worse at night. The woods were so thick that it was pitch black. Then I had the most terrifying experience ever. A thunderstorm! Every time the thunder boomed, the whole house shook. I grabbed the baby and hid under the bed. I was never in a thunderstorm in the country before. Every time there was a storm, I would hide under the bed or hide in the closet. I slowly got used to it, but it was hard, really hard.

It was also strange getting to know the people in that rural area. In the beginning the natives looked at us as a curious animal. Here come these newcomers, talking in funny languages like Yiddish and Polish, barely speaking English, and claiming to be equal Americans. The natives knew nothing of our background, whether we were educated, whether we were well-to-do. I think they thought all refugees were low class and ignorant because we were persecuted, or couldn't make a living in Europe. We came because we had no choice. We had no country. We had to go some place.

Eventually, we made many new friends, but it was difficult at first. I can say now that it is a wonderful thing to raise your children on a farm. But I'll let Sol tell that chapter of our story.

The top photo shows Goldie's and Sol's bungalow in the 1960s. The three children playing in the foreground are Sol and Goldie's children Joseph and Eve and friend. The bottom photo shows Sol and Goldie on their chicken farm around 1960.

# Part III

# Epilogue

# Chapter Fourteen

## Chicken Farmers

### (As told by Sol)

When we arrived in the United States in November, 1948, I was amazed by the absolute freedom of movement. You didn't have to carry an identification card. You didn't have to tell anybody where you're going, or why you're going, or what you're doing. If you have the money, you can go wherever you want. No borders. No passes. Nobody stops you. And the streets were very safe. In those days, you could walk at 3:00 in the morning in New York and nobody bothered you. If you wanted to eat, there was a restaurant open. If you wanted a cake, there was a bakery open. If you wanted milk, there was a store open. Life was so open and free. But the people born here had no idea what it meant to be free. I couldn't believe the freedom. Who could imagine a country where the Senator is Jewish?! Herbert Lehman. And Henry Morgenthau was a Secretary of the Treasury. And Felix Frankfurter was a Justice on the Supreme Court. All Jews! You could walk in New York City and speak Yiddish and nobody bothered you, or not speak Yiddish, and nobody bothered you. It was such an enormous feeling of absolute freedom and opportunity.

Three weeks after I came to New York, someone gave me my first job, as a Fuller brush man. I was eager to start. I went to the first door and knocked and a woman answered. When she heard my terrible English, she frowned and called me a "greenhorn." So I explained in Yiddish that I was a survivor of the concentration camps and had just come to America and couldn't speak English. When she heard my story, she took me door-to-door to every housewife in the whole apartment building—and she made every single one of them buy a Fuller brush from me!

So I started to make a little money. A dollar was a lot then. A quart of milk was 25 cents. A loaf of bread was 10 cents. A movie was a quarter. I paid 38 dollars a month for rent, which was too much for a cold-water walk-up with a bathroom in the hallway. But I had a happy time in New York because everybody was helpful. Non-Jews and Jews were helpful. Everybody was courteous and nobody pushed me around—except for one time.

It happened at a job at a furrier shop. I had tried two or three jobs but none of them lasted. This time I had just started working and all of the employees went on strike. They wanted to organize into a union, but I didn't understand. So I kept working. The next day this big guy, the union organizer, stopped me in the hallway and started to push me around.

"Look," I told him, "I survived Hitler, I'll survive you. You can't frighten me. You want to fight, we'll fight. But if you don't want to fight, just leave me be. I'll do what I want."

He stared at me and said, "You really want to fight?"

"Well, I really don't want to fight," I admitted, "but if you want to fight, I will." Then I pulled out a big pocketknife that I carried and said, "Now, you take it or I'll take it. Whoever wins. But you don't scare me."

I was young, just 23, and he looked at me differently. Then he said, "Okay. Come to the office with me, I'll give you a job."

"I don't want to come to your office to get a job," I replied. "I have a job."

Then I went upstairs to the furrier boss and I told him what happened. I said, "I'm sorry, but I'm quitting on Friday. I don't want to get between you and the union. I don't want to join the union. I don't want to fight the union either."

The furrier appreciated my offer and said, "Thanks. Work as long as you can."

So I went on to try another job. That first summer in New York City in 1949 was unbearably hot. So we went to the Catskill Mountains to escape for a while. After we came back, we moved into a new apartment on Claremont Avenue near Columbia University in a very nice neighborhood. A few weeks later, I went to High Holy Day services at a small synagogue on Kol Nidre night. The Rabbi was Orthodox and most of the worshippers were concentration camp survivors. It was the most memorable sermon I ever heard. The Rabbi said that God gave humans the capacity to remember and the capacity to forget. Certain things God wants you to remember. But it is also important to forget. If we had to live with our worst memories every day, we could not live a sane life. So we thank God for giving us the capacity to shut out certain memories.

I can see that Rabbi now. Small, wiry, with a red beard. He spoke to the whole congregation, but I thought he was talking just to me. He helped me to understand what I was feeling. It was more than four years after my father's death, but I would often think of the horrible times, and my guilt. I had bad memories in the day and bad dreams in the night. Sometimes I would have the shakes. It was too much to remember the painful memories day after day. The Rabbi's sermon told me it was okay to push the memories out. Not that I would forget forever, even if I tried to. But I did not have to live with it every day.

Life goes on. While we were poor and living on the Lower East Side, we had a friend named Noah Erlich, who worked for my father back in Poland. Mr. Erlich moved to Vineland in southern New Jersey. We heard that he was doing well as a chicken farmer, producing fresh eggs, and so my mother, brother and I took a trip to see for ourselves. It was the summer. It was beautiful. Green trees, sun, quiet, nice people. The town had many nice Italians and a few Jewish families. I fell in love with the idyllic country scene.

Mr. Erlich looked very happy. "It's wonderful here," he said. "You don't have to speak English. You don't have to talk to anybody. You get up in the morning. You eat your breakfast. You do your work. It's hard work, but at the end of the day, you made a good living."

Then we went to see another friend, Miles Lerman, who had also moved to Vineland. I knew his wife Krysia from my old neighborhood in Radom before the war. Her sister went to school with my sister. Miles was very happy, too. He had his own house and worked on his own land right outside the door.

It was almost too good to be true. At that time, eggs were under government price support so you were guaranteed a good income no matter what. You didn't need much money to get started and the Jewish Agricultural Society was giving out low interest loans for becoming farmers. You could get a big, big mortgage at low, low interest and buy a house and five acres of farmland for just $2,000 down. That's all it took. And there was another good reason to do it. The Korean War broke out in June, 1950. Somebody said if you worked on a farm, you would be exempt from the draft as an essential worker. This meant a lot to my mother. She had already lost her husband and two sons in the war in Europe, and she was not going to lose any more of her family in another war.

So, for just $2,000, we bought two chicken farms on Lake Road in Vineland, New Jersey—one for Joe, one for me, side by side. Shortly after, my sister Ann and her husband Norbert bought a third chicken farm, which was right next to ours on Bernard Road. The Finkelsteins were together again. We all used credit to get our farms started. First we used credit to hire someone to build our chicken coops; then we used credit to buy the chicken feed. Credit was easy to get because the Jewish farmers had already shown that they were honest and reliable in repaying their loans.

And you didn't have to go to college to become a chicken farmer. There wasn't too much to learn and there was always somebody willing to show you the ropes. Each farmer helped the other. When I came, the other chicken farmers helped me get started. When more newcomers came, I helped them get started. Chicken farming was not a competitive business because every chicken farmer was doing the same thing. So the Jewish chicken farmers were like a big extended family. It only took a year and a half to have a full flock of chickens and lots of eggs. Lo and behold, we were capitalists!

Vineland wasn't the only place that had Jewish chicken farmers. There was Lakewood and Toms River and Freehold, too. We organized ourselves as the Jewish Poultry Farmers Association of South Jersey, the JPFA, and I was elected the second President. In those days, everybody knew everybody. Everybody was friendly with everybody. If Harry had a baby boy, we would all go to his house for the *bris*. If Abe had a baby boy, we would all go to his house for the *bris*. It was not unusual to have a hundred and fifty people come to a *bris*. As we grew older and more established, the JPFA threw bigger, more sophisticated parties that were attended by five or six hundred people—and it was always with singing and dancing in Polish and Yiddish and Hebrew and English. There was a women's organization, too, called the Pioneer Women and they threw their famous Pioneer Picnics. Who could imagine that a group of urban, Jewish concentration camp survivors from cities in the Old World would rebuild a new Jewish community, as rural chicken farmers, in the New World?

We had two more children in Vineland. Joseph was born in 1952, and Eve several years later. Our son Joseph Simon Finkelstein was named after Goldie's father Joseph Cukier and Goldie's maternal grandfather Simon Goldstein. Our daughter Eve was named Marion Eve, after Goldie's mother Miriam and Goldie's maternal grandmother Chava (Eve) Szolowicz Goldstein.

My brother Joe and his wife Helen also had three children, Rochelle, Sandy and Barbara. They lived on one side of us, while my sister Ann and her husband Norbert (Natek) and their daughter Joanie lived on the other side of us. The seven cousins moved freely between our three farms, played with each other in all three yards, and ate meals in all three homes. We all cared for each other, six concentration camp survivors living together as one big family, raising a second generation of seven American children, and 20,000 chickens.

There were so many Jewish families with young children in Vineland in those days. In the summertime, the fathers would drive the mothers and children to Alliance Beach, which was a sandy stretch on a little river called the Maurice River. The beach was filled with people, sitting on beach blankets, catching sun, mothers with infants, little toddlers playing in the sand, children playing games, eating hot dogs, drinking sodas, and, of course, swimming. Back then, the river water was very clean. The boys loved to play a game called "buck buck," where they would all jump over each other's backs. There were so many people at the beach that they put up a building with refreshments. A pretzel was 2 cents. A pretzel with mustard was 3 cents. There were pinball machines inside, too, for 5 cents a game.

Of course, the men could not be at Alliance Beach all day. We had work to do—feed chickens, collect eggs, wash eggs, pack eggs. It was a nice routine. The men would bring their wives and children to the beach in the morning, go back to the farm, do the farm work, then come back for lunch, or a late afternoon meal. The men would talk about business and politics and gossip (men gossip too), sometimes until after dinner. At one time or another, I think almost everybody came to Alliance Beach to socialize.

Those were glorious days. We produced eggs on our chicken farm from 1951 until 1962. Gradually, we stopped farming and started to buy eggs from other farmers to process, freeze and sell directly to bakeries and commercial outlets. We were very successful, and the business grew and expanded to selling other farm products, too. Our business was called "Finkelstein Farms."

We found our Zion in New Jersey. It was the dream of Zionism preached by my older brothers, the dream that sustained me during the terrible years of the war. I knew how important it was to have Jewish pride and Jewish identity. That's why we sent our children to a Jewish school and that's why I founded a Zionist youth group for the Jewish kids in south Jersey. It was called Young Judaea and it's still going strong today.

I also wanted to do something to remember the victims of the Holocaust. In 1951 or 1952, I organized a Holocaust Memorial Day. About five hundred people came to the service. I think we were the first in the state, if not in the United States, to establish a day for Holocaust services. And we originated a format that has been copied all over. Six people would light six candles, one for each of the six million Jews murdered, and we would pray.

As time passed, however, chicken farming and the egg production business became more economically depressed. In the 1960's, more and more people began leaving the farming communities around Vineland to try new businesses. One did groceries in Philadelphia. Another did liquor stores in Washington. One did construction in Canada. Others went into real estate. And the next generation grew up and went off to college. By the 1970's, much of the Jewish chicken farming community around Vineland had dispersed.

# CHAPTER FIFTEEN

---

# An Extraordinary Deliverance

(As told by Sol)

*God has sent me ahead of you*
*To ensure your survival on earth*
*And to save your lives*
*In an extraordinary deliverance.*
*Genesis 45:7*

I remember once, around 1956, I traveled up to New York City to visit some friends. One of those friends had a cousin named Zalman, who was a Lubavitch Orthodox Jew. He said, "Sol, come with me to meet the Lubavitcher Rebbe."

Now this was a great honor. The Rebbe was a great famous Rabbi, a saintly man, and to meet him was something special. "Sure," I said.

So Zalman brought me into the room to meet the Lubavitcher Rebbe. I was just a poor chicken farmer from New Jersey, but I was meeting a great holy man in his private study.

"Where do you come from?" the Rebbe asked me.

"I come from Vineland," I said. "I am a survivor of the concentration camps. I was in Auschwitz and Mauthausen. I lost my father and my two brothers. Now I have a lovely wife and three wonderful children. And we live on a chicken farm in New Jersey."

I spoke to him for maybe two minutes. "Child," the Rebbe said in Yiddish, "You are destined to have nothing but heaven in life—because you have already been to hell." That was it. "*Gey gazunterheyt,*" he said with a kindly voice. "Go in good health." As short as could be. But it was something that I will never forget.

---

What the Rebbe said was so true. America has been a heaven to us. I have no complaints against God because as bitter as I had it in the war, I have had it sweet ever since. If not for the curse of war, I might have never met Goldie. As pretty as she is, she is much prettier on the inside. She is a loving and caring wife and mother. She blessed me with three wonderful children, Jacob, Joseph, and Eve. She created a Jewish home full of happiness and love. And now we have five wonderful grandchildren. What else does one need? The Hebrews have an expression. It's from Pirkei Avot 4:1. *Ezyeh-hu ashir?* Who is rich? *Ha'samayach bechelko.* The man who is happy with his lot.

Goldie and I lived our lives by focusing on the positive. Other than our annual Holocaust memorial service, we didn't talk about the war for many, many years. It was too painful. Most of our friends in Vineland were also Holocaust survivors, but nobody ever talked about it. We never knew if someone lost a sister or brother or parent or child or spouse. None of us knew. It was very curious. As a matter of fact, it was years before Goldie and I knew each other's stories. And we decided together not to tell our children until they were much older. We did not want to burden them with it. First of all, Goldie couldn't do it. She knew she would cry right away if she tried. She had nightmares about losing her family. She saw our children in the same situation. She didn't want them to be afraid of losing their parents. She didn't want them to have nightmares. So we protected our children from our past.

It's true that time heals a lot of things, but you never forget. Goldie described it like this: "Even now, almost sixty-five years later, the memories make me cry. When I talk about my past, I'm a little girl who lost her family and it's very sad. It still affects my life, absolutely. For me there is no closure. I'm not a psychologist, but I think it is because I never saw my parents killed. There's no grave. There's no eyewitness. I still don't like to talk about it. But if it helps others to tell my story, I am willing."

I think a little different than Goldie, maybe, but not quite. When you get to be my age, you know the inevitability of death. You're not going to live forever. Suppose something happens to you, you wouldn't want the memories to go unsaid. So I don't mind talking about the Holocaust as much as Goldie. It's true, when we got married in 1947, we never talked about the past with each other. It was too painful. And it was mutual. I wanted to protect Goldie and Goldie wanted to protect me. We were in love and happy. I didn't want our marriage to be clouded by misery. I didn't want to mar it with any sadness. It sounds corny, but Goldie and I have been married for 61 years. We've had a 61 year honeymoon, a continuous love affair. It's almost unbelievable that I'm an old man now.

But now, being old, we should tell our stories while we still can. People need to know what happened. We have to remember how bad it was so the Holocaust won't happen again.

Many people still ask why there was a Holocaust. Where was God when the six million Jews were slaughtered? Where was God when young children were murdered? Some say God wanted it that way. Some say there is no God because He wouldn't want it that way. I can only resolve it in my own way. I know there is a God because He saved me at least four times in the nick of time. And apparently God saved me for a purpose—to remember what happened, to teach others to remember, and to help bring Jewish life out of the ashes. And God gave me the best partner in the world to do it, my lovely wife, Goldie.

We are so proud that all of our children are Jewish-educated and spend a lot of time and money for Judaism. My sons have been Presidents and officers of their congregations and serve on the boards and as Presidents of a Jewish Day School, and other Jewish organizations, and the United Way. And they have raised their children Jewish. My oldest son Jack has two children, David and Ilana. And my second son Joseph has three children. The oldest one is Adam, Avrum Moshe in Hebrew, named after my oldest brother Abraham (Avrum) and my grandfather Moshe Warszenbrot; the middle one is Julie Miriam, Zahava Miriam in Hebrew, named after my mother Golda and my wife's mother, Miriam; and the youngest is Seth Aaron, Shmuel Aaron, named after his mother's grandfather Samuel and my older brother Aaron. All of my grandchildren know how to *daven*; they say a beautiful *Maftir* and they can *daven* a *Mussaf* and a *Shacharit*. Even the youngest one can sing *Havdalah* like nobody's business.

Our children, their spouses and our grandchildren give us so much *nachas*, pride. My oldest son, Jacob, who was named after my father, is a Professor at the University of Rochester School of Medicine in biochemistry. He has lectured all over the world and is a consultant to the Atomic Energy Commission. My second son Joseph, who was named after Goldie's father and grandfather, is a full partner in a very prestigious law firm in Philadelphia. And my daughter Eve is a paralegal and a wonderful singer. As a matter of fact, she sang at our 45th wedding anniversary. Maybe, God willing, she'll sing at our 75th!

I am reminded again of the Hebrew expression, "*Netzach Yisrael lo ishaker.*" The Jewish people will never cease. We are the proof of it. We rose from the ashes of war and the death pits of the concentration camps. It is unbelievable that it happened. We were determined to survive and not allow the enemy to eliminate Jewish life. We were reduced to nothing, yet we overcame with our humanity intact. We made it, and we made it for our children. "*Netzach Yisrael lo ishaker,*" the Jewish people will never cease. *Amen.*

This photo from 1962 shows the grand occasion of Sol and Goldie's first son becoming a bar mitzvah, the first in the Finkelstein family since Sol's bar mitzvah in 1938. *Netzach Yisrael lo ishaker*—"The Jewish people will never cease."

# AFTERWORD

## by Joseph S. Finkelstein

On May 5 of each year, my father, Sol Finkelstein, declares, "Today is my birthday." Although he was born in September, Sol counts the start of his life from May 5, 1945, the day he was liberated from Mauthausen concentration camp. On that date, my father emerged from a stack of corpses under which he had been hiding from the Nazis—and he literally rose from the dead. He felt that his old life ceased to exist and a new Sol was born.

Goldie Cukier Finkelstein, my mother, never speaks about what happened during the war, unless I ask her direct questions, and then with great reluctance. One day, however, she surprised me by saying, "The girl who was Goldie in Europe died over there, I am not that person, I am somebody else."

Both of my parents rebuilt their lives after the Holocaust as new people. They decided that they would not burden their children, nor to the extent possible, their own marriage with painful memories of the past. So, as the second-generation children of survivors, my siblings and I grew up in America without knowledge of the life and death events that our parents had experienced in Europe. Nor did we dare to ask because we sensed that raising the subject would cause pain and open old wounds. The harrowing stories contained in this book were utter secrets to us until we were grown adults in our thirties. Until then, we knew almost nothing of the events that had shaped our parents' past lives and which have silently shaped our own as part of our family history and identity.

We knew a few things, of course, like the names of our missing grandparents. We knew that our parents had lost siblings, our missing aunts and uncles, but we knew nothing of substance about who they were, or what had happened to them. We knew the names of a few Polish towns, like Sosnowiec and Radom. If we asked where my parents were during the war, we heard the names of "Auschwitz" and "Bergen-Belsen"—but without explanation or elaboration of what happened to them there. There were no details as to how they were mistreated or how they survived. We also could see the number tattooed on my father's forearm, which was scary, and never explained, except that "the Nazis did it to me."

We sensed that something enormous and terrible had happened to our parents in Europe, something so horrible that no one could talk about it. It was never a stated rule, we just knew it was that way.

The stories, memories and histories in this book were learned over decades, in stages, or perhaps more accurately, in layers. I first learned the basic stories in 1989, more than forty-four years after the fact, in connection with a "New Life/New Leadership" tribute dinner by the State of Israel Bonds. I was already 37 years old. The chairman of the event asked my parents to tell their stories, something that I was unable to do, and I learned a little bit of what had happened for the first time. The stories made me enormously sad and were (and still are) very upsetting, but I was also amazed at the strength and resilience of my parents and their refusal to surrender to the Nazis or to despair. Five years later, in 1994, my father (but not my mother) agreed to be interviewed as part of the "Transcending Trauma" research project associated with the Penn Council on Relationships, which was researching how Holocaust survivors recovered from the shock and loss and rebuilt their lives and families. Two years later, both of my parents participated in video interviews as part of the Shoah Foundation project to record the eyewitness accounts of Holocaust survivors. Then, in 1998 and 1999, my parents and I, and other family members were interviewed as subjects in a documentary feature film called *The Phoenix Effect*, which examines the intergenerational impact of the Holocaust (www.phoenixdocumentary.com).

With each successive retelling by my parents, I learned new details and events. I still did not break the unspoken family rule of silence, but I could listen as my parents told their traumatic stories to third parties in a safe, allowable setting. Without having to directly ask the questions myself, I was gradually finding answers to a mysterious hidden past that had affected me so profoundly.

This book came about, in part, because of my desire to collect and organize the stories, memories, histories and feelings that had been articulated in bits and pieces, for different purposes, and in different forms of media, over several decades. My parents had always said they wished they could write their stories, and felt the necessity of leaving a legacy of their experiences to their family and to future generations. I also felt a necessity to gather and preserve this information, and to ask my parents about it while I could do so. Fortunately, I met Jerry Jennings, a talented and committed writer, who helped several survivors write and publish their memoirs, and he said he would be willing to do the same for my parents.

It was obvious, however, that despite the existence of prior interviews and collected information, there were many details never revealed. This time, unlike the prior interviews, I asked questions myself. At times, it was difficult to put my parents through pain by asking them to recall details, clarify events, or remember people, but they understood what I was trying to do, and that I needed to do it, and they endured it and remembered a great amount of detail, in surprising accuracy.

Beyond personal memories, I wanted to make this book as historically accurate as possible. In 2007, original historical records became available to me, which had been held since the war by the International Red Cross. Largely inaccessible prior to that time, it was possible to search through documents and sources at the United States Holocaust Memorial Museum and Israel's Yad Vashem museum. In 2008, I traveled to Poland to visit my parents' home towns and found their childhood homes in Radom and Sosnowiec. I found cousins of my father in Israel, who had recorded some of the family history from Poland. I explored the archives at Auschwitz. I corresponded with kind people and helpful cemetery officials in Wels, Austria. My research enabled me to verify and discover facts and details that were unknown even to my parents, including the dates of prisoner transports, arrival dates at different camps, and lists of prisoners in which their names appear. Most significant of all, I discovered the final events and fate of my father's father, Jacob Finkelstein, which had been unknown to my father since the tragic day they were separated at Mauthausen, just a week before liberation.

In an emotional meeting, I began telling my father about the discovery by explaining how I had uncovered information about his father while searching for records about him. These records revealed what happened to Jacob and that there was a grave. I explained that Jacob had survived the march to Gunskirchen, but died in a hospital a few days after liberation, and that he was buried in a cemetery in Wels, Austria.

I then showed my father photographs of the Wels cemetery monument to the victims of Gunskirchen and the new Memorial built in 2001, which listed the known names of the 1,035 who died after liberation and were buried there. Then I showed him a blown up photograph of the Wels memorial wall on which he could clearly see his father's name engraved: Jakob Finkelstein.

My father was deeply moved. "This washes away all the guilt I've had," he said with a sigh. "I always felt responsible for my father's death. I thought he died because I left him alone and there was no one to care for him. Now I know that he was cared for, and died in a hospital, and it wasn't my fault." He went on to say that he could finally observe his father's *Yahrzeit* properly, the anniversary date of a deceased loved one, because he finally knew that May 8 was the true date of his father's death.

Later that day, my father said to my sister, "I can't tell you how many years I carried this with me. This lifts a great weight. Is it okay if I cry?"

"Of course," she said.

"But it is not sad tears," he explained, "It is actually tears of happiness. I'm happy that I now know what happened and that it wasn't my fault . . . ."

Today there is an individual gravestone above Jacob Finkelstein's final resting place, which we placed there while this book was being completed.

After their liberation from the concentration camps, Sol and Goldie felt that they were born again as new persons, with a new life and spirit. They talked of their previous lives in Europe as the lives of "different persons." In truth, they are the same people, who once lived happily in warm, loving Jewish families and vibrant communities in a world that has disappeared. The Jewish pride and values that they learned as children did not die in the Nazi concentration camps. My parents could easily be bitter for what was stolen from them and the cruelties done to them, but that would be the opposite of their values. My parents practice love, not hate; compassion, not bitterness; generosity and charity, not selfishness and materialism. They act with justice, honesty, and integrity. They prize human rights and human dignity. In a word, Sol and Goldie are each a "*Mensch*," a caring, sensitive, aware person, who acts with compassion for other people and concern for his or her community.

How was it possible for children like Sol and Goldie to endure such unimaginable horrors and losses, without once losing their own humanity, and go on to rebuild their lives and start new families?

The answer, I believe, is that they refused to surrender to despair—no matter how terrible the circumstances—and chose to live, as *Menschen*. When the only choice given to a Jew was death, Sol and Goldie each chose life, and after liberation, they made that same choice, each and every day. They chose life, not death, blessing, not curse (Deuteronomy 30:19).

As the next generation, we rejoice in the choices and courage of Sol and Goldie. We strive to live by the same Jewish values and *menschlichkeit* that carried them through seven years of unrelenting darkness. As parents, my wife Sara and I are thrilled to see their legacy is blazing bright in our own three children. Perhaps, by capturing my parents' stories in this book, we are extending their legacy of courage, love and hope to a broader world.

Photograph, 1999, the occasion of the Bat Mitzvah of granddaughter Ilana, from left to right: grandson David, oldest son Jacob, grandson Seth, second son Joseph, Sol, Goldie, son-in-law Craig, granddaughter Ilana, daughter-in-law Sara, daughter Eve, granddaughter Julie, daughter-in-law Gail and grandson Adam.

Photograph, 2003, graduation of grandson Seth from Perelman Jewish Day School, from left to right: grandson Seth, Goldie, Sol, granddaughter Julie, and grandson Adam.

# A Note From The Writer

## by Jerry L. Jennings

One day, when I was about seven years old, I discovered a small paperback book belonging to one of my older siblings. The cover was black with scary barbed wire letters scrawled across the top: "A U S C H W I T Z." Beneath the barbed wired letters, there was a black-and-white photograph of contorted bodies, shriveled and bony white, packed so tightly together that you couldn't tell which arms and legs belonged to whom. The silent, skull-like faces seemed to be crying out in great agony. I stared at the picture in horrified fascination. Since it was an adult book, I struggled to make sense of the words on the front and back cover: "Jews", "Nazis", "Auschwitz", "death camp." I gathered that some terrible people called Nazis did horrible, unspeakable things to kill millions of Jewish people. I could not fathom why anyone could commit such brutality.

Over the years, I often returned to stare at that book cover. I would read the scary words and slip into a suspended state of dark wonder. I never talked about it to anyone. For reasons I couldn't explain, I sensed that I, a Christian boy in upstate New York, was somehow connected to these tortured people, and that, if I could understand this hellish thing, I might understand something essential about human beings. I was imprinted by my discovery, bound to the Jewish people by a glue of mysterious and immeasurable sorrow.

Many decades later, I married a Jew, then became a Jew myself, and we have raised our children as Jews. I have enjoyed a blessed life. I am happy and grateful for having my deepest wishes fulfilled. On one memorable day, I was feeling that overflow of gratitude and wishing to give back, so I said a little prayer: "Please, God, use me for some purpose." A few days later, I found myself speaking with Stella Yollin, a Holocaust survivor, who was frustrated that she could not write well enough to record her story. I knew this was the sacred task

I had asked for. I had the rare privilege of researching, writing and publishing her incredible story as *Stella's Secret* (Xlibris, 2005). Within a week of completing Stella's book, I met Ida Firestone, another survivor, who also wanted her story told. Two years later, *Darkness Hides the Flowers* (Xlibris, 2007) was published, combining Ida's paintings and poetry with the narrative of her ordeals with the Gestapo in rural France.

*I Choose Life* is my third effort to honor and preserve the extraordinary stories of Jewish survivors of the Holocaust. I worry about the lost opportunity to record these stories while time allows. Survivors who were children and youth in 1945 are now in their late 70's and 80's. Through a psychological quirk of history, the most malicious and concentrated terror in human history was followed by an enormous silence. With a few notable exceptions, few survivors wanted to bear witness with their stories; and fewer people were inclined to listen. Sadly, the vast majority of survivors have passed away without breaking their silence. Their stories are gone, as irretrievable as the wind that ripples the grass over the cinder-fields of the murdered multitudes. It is only recently that the Holocaust has received appropriate attention and that survivors have been encouraged to speak.

Like most survivors, Sol and Goldie Finkelstein were silent, too, for most of their lives. Like anyone who awakens from a nightmare, they shunned the grotesque, writhing images and tried to shake off the prickles of terror. They feared that remembering too much might condemn them to a poisoned existence, dragging the chains of the past like some Dickens ghost. Sol and Goldie rarely, if ever, spoke of their traumas, even with each other, and consciously chose to withhold their history from their own children for fear of hurting them. No one can judge the wisdom or necessity of their silence. Surely, it was both wise and necessary, and so much more, because, in writing this book, Sol and Goldie taught me the depth of the struggle between remembrance and forgetting. Certain tragedies and losses are so profound, so total, that they are seared into the flesh of the victims' minds, while other experiences are so horrific that they must be sealed away in the crypts of the psyche. Recalling the details of a great trauma always threatens to re-open old wounds. To tell their stories, Sol and Goldie summoned the courage to re-open their wounds by returning to childhoods in which their dearest bonds—brothers, sisters, parents, grandparents, friends, loved ones—and their innocence—were all brutally ripped away. As Sol says, "a sane person cannot imagine what it was like." To dwell on such loss is unbearable, but to forget has the dreadful cost of preventing healing and closure.

Ultimately, Sol and Goldie agreed to tell their stories because they were asked to do so by their son Joe. It was as simple as that, yet painfully difficult for Sol and Goldie, and for Joe. They were willing because they understood that it was vitally important to Joe and their other children and grandchildren.

Certainly, Sol and Goldie had other reasons, too. They feel the responsibility to give tribute to family members who were killed; to bear witness to genocide; to help ensure that Jewish life will continue to thrive; and to educate the world so that this gargantuan tragedy will never be repeated.

Judaism was the reason for their persecution, but it was Judaism that helped Sol and Goldie survive through unendurable conditions. Sol was the recipient of multiple miracles and is certain that God personally intervened to save his life on several occasions. The pride and values that Sol gained from his Zionist youth groups and Jewish upbringing were crucial to retaining his humanity and hope. Sol literally rose from the bones of the dead with a blazing passion to renew Jewish life. He advocated for Jewish renewal in the Stuttgart Displaced Persons camp and, in 1955, Sol was the prime mover in starting a South Jersey chapter of a Jewish youth group program called Young Judaea. More than fifty years later, Sol's grandson Seth became the National Mazkir (President) of Young Judaea, and in the summer of 2008, Seth served as the camp counselor at Young Judaea's Camp Tel Yehudah for a bunk of twelve Jewish boys. One of those boys was my son Isaac. It must be another miracle of sorts, that the Zionist passion of one Jewish boy from Poland, born a generation before me, and a world apart, could directly touch my life and my son almost sixty years later.

I have no doubt of the Divine presence in this endeavor. I am humbled to be entrusted with this sacred task—to use my talents as a writer, historian and psychologist to convey stories of the Shoah with the most clarity, richness and effect that I can. I fervently hope that my efforts may also provide some closure and healing to the survivors. Sol and Goldie are pure diamonds. To sit at their table has made me rich.

## Sol's history

| Date | Age | Event |
| --- | --- | --- |
| Sept. 16, 1925 | 0 | Born in Pulawy, Poland on Rosh Hashanah. |
| Sept. 3, 1939 | G | Germans invade Poland. |
| Sept. 8, 1939 | 13 | Germans occupy Radom, Poland. |
| Fall 1939 | G | People grabbed off streets of Radom for forced labor. |
| Nov. 1939 | 14 | Father and brothers flee to Lvov in the Russian occupied zone of Poland. Abraham and Aaron teach Hebrew to children somewhere outside city. |
| Dec. 18, 1940 | G | First deportation of 1,840 Jews from Radom, mostly non-workforce families with elderly, sick and children. |
| March 1941 | G | 32,000 Radom Jews ordered into the "big" and "small" Radom ghettos. Ghettos are sealed on April 7, 1941. |

## Goldie's history

| Date | Age | Event |
| --- | --- | --- |
| Aug. 3, 1929 | 0 | Born in Haifa, Israel. Family moves back to Sosnowiec in Poland shortly afterward. |
| Sept.4, 1939 | 10 | Germans occupy Sosnowiec, Poland. |
| | G | People grabbed off streets of Sosnowiec for forced labor. |
| Nov.–Dec. 1939 | G | Germans expropriate Jewish businesses, appoint German administrators over Jewish businesses—including Goldie's father's store. |
| Nov. 1940 | G | Germans establish a transit camp in Sosnowiec for deportation to work camps. |

**Key: "G" denotes a "general" historical event**

| Sol's history | | | Goldie's history | | |
|---|---|---|---|---|---|
| Date | Age | Event | Date | Age | Event |
| Winter 1941 | 14 | Sol and Joe get jobs as mechanics for Air Force (*Luftwaffe*) at garage near Radom ghetto. Mother and sister Ann work for *Wehrmacht* in Radom. | 1941 | 11 | Germans empty out Goldie's father's dry goods store. |
| June 22, 1941 | G | Germans attack Russians in Russian-occupied Poland. Lvov captured by Germans July 2, 1941. | 1942–1943 | 11 | Goldie works in German factory, painting ceramic tile; sister Toby works for *Wehrmacht* company making knapsacks. |
| July 25–28, 1941 | 14 | Brothers Abraham and Aaron probably murdered by Ukrainians in "Petlura Days" pogroms in Lvov. | | | |
| | | | May 10, 1942 | 12 | First large scale deportation of 1,500 Jews from Sosnowiec to extermination at Auschwitz. |
| | | | June 1942 | G | Another 2,000 deported from the Sosnowiec area to Auschwitz, including residents of an old-age home and orphanage. |
| August 6–8, 1942 | G | SS surround the two ghettos and liquidate the smaller "Glinice" Radom ghetto. 6,000 sent to gas chambers at Treblinka. | August 12, 1942 | 13 | Every Jew in Sosnowiec (about 22,000) sent to central square/transit camp for selection. Goldie and family allowed to return home. |

| Sol's history | | | Goldie's history | | |
|---|---|---|---|---|---|
| Date | Age | Event | Date | Age | Event |
| August 16-18, 1942 | G | SS liquidate the big Radom ghetto. Sol and brother Joe saved by *Luftwaffe*; mother and sister saved by Herr Baker. 20,000 more Jews sent to be gassed at Treblinka. Only 2,000 remain in Radom. | August 12–18, 1942 | 13 | 8,000 Jews sent from Sosnowiec central square/transit camp to death at Auschwitz. |
| Mid/late Aug 1942 | 15 | Sister and mother moved to barracks to live and work on Wsola work farm outside Radom. Sol and Joe get jobs in munitions factory. | | | |
| Late August 1942 | 15 | Sol seized from streets within Radom ghetto by SS Commandant to be his personal car mechanic. | | | |
| Oct/Nov 1942 | 16 | Sol nearly executed for false accusations of stealing gas. Sol joins family on the Wsola work farm. Mother bribes SS to bring father back from Lvov to rejoin family. | October 1942 | G | Sosnowiec ghetto established in Srodula suburb, but Goldie's family remains in their own apartment. Transfer of Jews into Srodula ghetto continued through March 1943. |
| December 1942 | 16 | Germans liquidate the Wsola workfarm and move the family to Pionki munitions factory labor camp. | | | |

| Sol's history | | | Goldie's history | | |
|---|---|---|---|---|---|
| Date | Age | Event | Date | Age | Event |
| | | | Feb—March 1943 | 13 | Goldie and sister Toby seized off street; Sister sent home, Goldie sent to Gogolin transit camp, then to Graeben work camp (a Gross-Rosen subcamp). Goldie works in flax factory. |
| April 19, 1943 | G | Warsaw ghetto uprising begins. | June 22-24, 1943 | G | 1,200 Sosnowiec Jews sent to Auschwitz for extermination. |
| | | | August 1-16, 1943 | 14 | Sosnowiec ghetto liquidated. 15,000 Jews, including Goldie's family, sent to Auschwitz on last transport. |
| Spring 1944 | 18 | Pionki changes from labor camp to concentration camp. | February 1944 | 14 | Graeben camp changes from work camp to concentration camp run by SS. |
| June 6, 1944 | G | D-day—Allied forces land in Normandy. | | | |

| Sol's history | | | Goldie's history | | |
|---|---|---|---|---|---|
| Date | Age | Event | Date | Age | Event |
| July 31, 1944 | 18 | SS evacuate Sol and family and 3,000 prisoners from Pionki as Russian Army approaches. Train arrives at Auschwitz where 1,000 immediately killed in gas chambers. Mother and sister separated from father, Sol and Joe. | | | |
| Early August 1944 | 18 | Sol, Joe and father transferred to nearby Sosnowiec-II subcamp. Sol works on anti-aircraft guns. Father suffers from melting furnace. | | | |
| Jan. 17, 1945 | 19 | Sol escapes execution for stolen linens because SS evacuate Sosnowiec II in face of advancing Russian Army. The death march begins. | Early Feb 1945 | 15 | Germans evacuate the Graeben camp because Russian army approaching. Death march in snow to reach cattle cars. |
| Jan 31, 1945 | 19 | Death march through freezing cold arrives at Wodzislaw train station where they board cattle car train to Mauthausen concentration camp. | | | |
| February 2, 1945 | 19 | Sol, Joe and Jakob arrive at Mauthausen concentration camp. Sol and Joe bury 600 dead Russian officers. | mid Feb 1945 | 15 | Arrives at Bergen-Belsen. One week later Goldie picked to work in SS "Watchtower" subcamp outside main camp. |

| Sol's history | | | Goldie's history | | |
|---|---|---|---|---|---|
| Date | Age | Event | Date | Age | Event |
| March 7, 1945 | 19 | Sol, Joe and father and 200 men sent by train ride to Hinterbrühl camp, a secret underground mine that housed a V2 rocket and jet aircraft factory. | | | |
| April 1-8, 1945 | 19 | Sol and 1884 prisoners make death march back to Mauthausen from Hinterbrühl. Put in quarantine block for 4 days. Sol and Joe become "Prominents." | Mid Apr. 1945 | 15 | In middle of typhus epidemic, Goldie sick with typhus and dysentery, but saved by Dr. Bimko. |
| April 16 & 26 | G | SS begin deporting mostly Hungarian Jews from the Mauthausen tent camp. | Apr. 15, 1945 | G | Bergen-Belsen liberated on first day of Passover. |
| April 28, 1945 | 19 | Father is deported with last of the Jews from the tent camp to Gunskirchen concentration camp. | | | |
| May 4, 1945 | 19 | Father survives to see liberation on May 4, but is already deathly ill. | May-Dec. 1945 | 15 | After recovery, Goldie lives in hospital at Bergen Belsen DP camp with 3 nurse/sisters. |

| | Sol's history | | | Goldie's history | |
|---|---|---|---|---|---|
| Date | Age | Event | Date | Age | Event |
| May 5, 1945 | 19 | Sol and Joe narrowly escape execution by hiding in pile of corpses. Mauthausen liberated by Patton's 11th Army at 11am. | | | |
| May 8, 1945 | 19 | Father dies in hospital in Wels. | | | |
| late June to Sept. 1945 | 19 | Sol moved to Gusen US Army hospital to recover. | | | |
| Sept. 1945 | 20 | Joe goes back to Poland to reunite with mother and sister in Lodz. Sol still too weak to travel. | | | |
| October 1945 | 20 | Sol and Joe travel to Lodz to reunite with mother and sister. | | | |
| October 1945 | 20 | Family takes train to Prague to stay in refugee hotel for 3 weeks. Joe quarantined in hospital for another 2 months. Sol stays; family goes on to Stuttgart DP camp. | | | |
| Nov. 1945 | 20 | Sol arrives in Stuttgart to rejoin family. | | | |

| Sol's history | | | Goldie's history | | |
|---|---|---|---|---|---|
| Date | Age | Event | Date | Age | Event |
| March 29, 1946 | 21 | Jews in Stuttgart DP Camp riot after German police raid on black marketers kills Jewish man. | Early 1946 | 16 | Goldie moves to Stuttgart with Frania and Sam Zimmerman; works as dental assistant for Sam's brother Karl. |
| Jan/Feb 1947 | 21 | Taking train from Stuttgart to Munich, he meets Goldie on her way to visit friend with TB in sanatorium. | | 17 | |
| March 1947 | 21 | Re-encounters Goldie in Stuttgart; Goldie is student in Sol's Hebrew class. | | 17 | |
| | | | July 1947 | 18 | Goldie prevented by Frania from boarding the ship *Exodus 1947*, which leaves France on July 11, 1947, carrying about 4,500 Jewish emigrants. |
| Nov. 17, 1947 | 22 | Sol and Goldie married (same day as Queen of England). | | 18 | |
| Nov. 18, 1948 | 23 | Boat to America, land in Boston on almost 1st wedding anniversary. | | 19 | |
| Jan. 1949 | 23 | Living on Lower East Side in NYC; first son born in March. | | 19 | |
| August 1951 | 24 | Move to Vineland to become chicken farmers. | | 21 | |

# ACKNOWLEDGEMENTS

I wish to thank Joseph Finkelstein and the entire Finkelstein family for the wonderful privilege of getting to know Sol and Goldie and to honor them with this book; to my fellow members of the Wynnewood Writers Group (Barbara Cohen-Kligerman, Sharon Sorokin, Elaine Crauderueff and Miriam Camitta) for feedback and ideas that have enhanced the book; to my mother, Thelma Jennings, who taught me the importance of humility and service to others; and to my wife Jane, whose loving support enriches and sustains me, even when my work on projects like this steals time away from her—and for being the very best editor of my words and integrity.

Jerry L. Jennings

I would like to extend thanks to the researchers of the United States Holocaust Memorial Museum in Washington, D.C. (Randolph Davis, Molly Abramowitz, and William Connelly) and Yad Vashem in Jerusalem, Israel, for securing and explaining historical records of the Finkelstein and Cukier families from the International Red Cross archives and elsewhere; to Mrs. Charlotte Lugmayr-Frantz in Austria, for locating the grave of Jakob Finkelstein in Wels cemetery; to Mrs. Gabriella Puehringer, administrator of the municipal cemetery in Wels, Austria, for obtaining and placing a grave marker above the grave of Jakob Finkelstein; to Mr. Guenter Kalliauer, archivist of the City of Wels, for providing research information; to Betty Meitner, for furnishing photographs of my parents in the Stuttgart DP camp; to Dr. David Engel of New York University, and Alex Ebel and Maureen Higgins, for translating German and Hebrew documents; to Ellen Chodosh for her editorial suggestions; to my assistant Bernadette Currie, for her dedication; to my cousin Rochelle Finkelstein Porter for furnishing her father Joseph Finkelstein's written recollections; to my sister, Eve Finkelstein Thomas, for her encouragement; to Dr. Jerry Jennings, for his commitment, sensitivity, and enthusiasm; and to my wife Sara Finkelstein, for her many editorial suggestions and contributions, and her support, patience and love.

Joseph S. Finkelstein

CPSIA information can be obtained
at www.ICGtesting.com
Printed in the USA
BVHW032057120719
553336BV00001B/5/P

9 781441 503053